Martha
Thanks f
Pat T

CW00819780

Turning 60— Prematurely

Memories of a Boy Growing Up

Patrick Triplett

PublishAmerica
Baltimore

First printing

PublishAmerica has allowed this work to remain exactly as the author intended, verbatim, without editorial input.

ISBN: 978-1-4489-8830-3
PUBLISHED BY PUBLISHAMERICA, LLLP
www.publishamerica.com
Baltimore

Printed in the United States of America

About the Book:

This is a story about my life, told from the heart, about a boy who gradually, yet suddenly, became an old man.

It is a collection of memories of a person born in the baby boomer generation, beginning when I was six, recalling all of the thrills, spills, adventures, and misadventures of a boy who grew into adulthood, and would eventually experience a traumatic episode that would change the course of my life.

The events that take place in this story are true to the best of my recollection. It is a roller coaster of a ride, from my early days as Superman, to my days as Old Man.

Patrick Triplett

This book is dedicated to the memory of my father, to my mother, my three sons, and especially to my wife, who has put up with me every day for all these years.

Chapter 1

~

There are significant birthdays in everyone's life, like 16, when you qualify for your driver's license, and 21, when you get to drink legally. But for me, there are two that have a definite stigma attached to them. One is 30. The other is 60.

When you turn 30, you have officially crossed over a line. You can no longer get away with doing stupid things and blame it on youth. 30 means you have to act like a responsible adult, whether you are ready or not. It means you need to try harder for that promotion at work, in order to make more money for saving up for things, like the kids college education and your retirement fund.

When you hit 60, people start giving you discounts and free stuff, because they realize you are old and they feel sorry for you, and it's their way of making you feel special.

I have now passed both marks. The first one hit me hard. The second one floored me like a ton of bricks.

You hear of people aging gracefully into their twilight years? We'll, I'm going in kicking and screaming. I'm not supposed to be 60. I'm still supposed to be in my 20's, or 30's, or 40's. I'll even take 50. At least all my parts still worked then.

What happened? How did I get to this point all of a sudden? I can still remember the day I turned six as if it were yesterday.

It was November of 1954. I was playing with my best friend Roddy Martin in his back yard when his mother came out and said hi and asked me how I was doing. "I'm six," I said proudly, only to have her tell me I'd better go home. And so I did, naturally dejected and confused. When I got home and told my mom she immediately figured out that my friend's mom must have thought I said that I was sick, not six, a logical explanation considering I was missing most of my front teeth and as a result talked with a bit of a lisp.

It's funny the things you retain from your childhood days and the things you forget. I clearly remember my first day of kindergarten at Longfellow Elementary in Clinton, Iowa, proudly wearing my yellow Roy Rogers shirt with the tassels on the sleeves only to have a classmate throw up all over it.

And I vividly remember my first day of grade school. I had to take the city bus because the tiny Catholic school I attended, Saint Mary's, did not have a bus. We were a one-car family back then and the plan was that my dad would drop me off on his way to work and I would take the city bus home after school.

We practiced the routine for what seemed like half the summer. We would walk up the steps to the front door, walk back down and then over to the bus stop at the corner. We did it so many times that I could do it in my sleep. My dad dropped me off on my first day and we went over it one more time. Piece of cake. No problem.

Then came the glitch. After school was over our teacher led us out the door. Unfortunately it was the back door, not the front, not the one we had practiced a hundred times. I walked down the steps and stood at the corner. For hours.

I don't recall panicking or wondering why I was the only one at the corner or why the bus hadn't come by to pick me up. I just kept standing there waiting. Finally my uncle Bob drove by and asked me what I was doing.

"Waiting for the bus," I replied.

"Well, you've got a long wait," he said. "Hop in."

My mom was naturally upset and had called him and asked him to go looking for me. I finally arrived safely home and into the arms of my relieved mom. Needless to say, we practiced going out the back door from then on.

And I remember the two-block walk from where the bus dropped me off to our house. I recall walking past one of the houses along the way one day and seeing a bright red sign that read "Quarantine."

I didn't know what that meant and asked my mom about it. She said it meant that someone in that house was very ill and that people should not go near them.

From that day on every time I passed that house I held my

breath so as not to contract the mysterious illness that lay inside. Eventually the sign was taken down and I could breathe normally again.

But the one memory above all the others in those early days was the saddle that they sold at the local Sears store. It wasn't a plastic saddle on a wooden horse that you stuck a dime in and rode around in circles. It was a real saddle, mounted on a post, made of genuine leather with the big horn, reins and stirrups, and for the five minutes or so that I was able to sit on it until either my parents or the store manager made me get off, I was either Roy Rogers or the Lone Ranger, my two favorite cowboy heroes. I mounted and dismounted that saddle just like I saw them do it on TV and in the movies a hundred times.

Like most boys my age I had my heroes. Besides the cowboys there was Robin Hood. I had the green outfit, including the pointy hat with the feather and my trusty bow and arrows, rubber tipped to keep me from accidentally wounding a family member or neighbor. My younger sister Ellen was usually my No. 1 target. She was the evil Sheriff of Nottingham, whether she wanted to be or not, and was struck many times by Robin's ever accurate arrows.

But as heroes went, Superman was clearly No. 1 in those early days. Not only did I watch every episode on TV religiously, with George Reeves playing my hero, I also had the outfit, the blue shirt and pants with the big red "S" on the chest and the red cape. I even had the boots to complete the wardrobe. I wore it every day it seemed, and probably slept in it at night. I even remember the day I got it. My mom told me there was a package on the front door step and that it was for me.

"Where did it come from?" I asked.

"Superman must have flown by and dropped if off for you," my mom replied, trying her best to act serious.

Then there was "the Superman game" that we played what seemed like every night after dinner. Actually it was my parents who were playing. For me it was quite serious. The way it went was I would dress up as Clark Kent, (mild mannered reporter), wearing an old pair of my dad's glasses, an old hat of his and a sport coat. My parents would sit on the couch together while I sat in a chair, none of us saying a word until inevitably one of them would say, "That Superman is such a sissy. He's not nearly as tough as he thinks he is." At which point I would stand up to leave the room.

"Where are you going, Clark?" one of them would ask.

"I have to go do something," I would reply, and walked upstairs to my room. Pretty soon I reappeared, running down the steps, leaping the last three or four and standing in front of my parents in full Superman garb. With fists clenched against my hips and a stern look on my face, I said, "Sissy, huh? I'll show you who's a sissy," as I grabbed them by their heads and knocked them together, rendering them "unconscious" and restoring the reputation of my superhero.

Besides Superman, the Lone Ranger, and Robin Hood, my favorite TV shows back then were **Howdy Doody, Captain Kangaroo** and **Gabby Hayes.** And then there were the Saturday morning cartoon shows, like **Bugs Bunny,**

Daffy Duck, Mickey Mouse, Tom and Jerry, Huckleberry Hound, Mighty Mouse, and last but not least, **Popeye the Sailor Man**. I tried my best to eat spinach right out of the can like he did to make me strong, but always gagged on every bite. It would have been much easier on me if he had gained his strength from eating cookies or ice cream.

When I wasn't busy playing one of my heroes or watching my favorite TV shows, I would spend my days building things in our basement, from buses to airplanes to escalators to automatic pin setters.

Despite the fact I had no clue what I was doing, nor the equipment necessary to make any of these things other than what my dad had in his workshop, I would spend hours a day trying.

I was fascinated by the way the city bus doors automatically opened to let the passengers in and tried to make them myself with whatever I could find lying around the basement. When that didn't work I moved on. I spent what seemed like weeks attempting to build an airplane. Not a toy airplane or even a model one. A real airplane that I could fly. A bi-plane, with the two wings like the kind they flew in World War I that I once saw in a movie. What I don't recall is, even if I were able to build one, how I would manage to get it out of the basement. But I wasn't about to let a trivial thing like that stop me.

And there was the escalator that I used to ride on at the Van Allen department store downtown. I was fascinated by the fact that you could stand on a step and be transported up and down floors without having to move. I tried my best to make one of my own at home, but alas, it too ended in failure.

Despite never being successful in my attempts, the strange thing is I don't ever remember getting upset or discouraged. I just eventually would give up and move on to the next project. In the case of the automatic pin setter, I did succeed in one respect. Even though I failed miserably once again in trying to build one, I managed to provide my parents with the biggest laugh I ever heard out of them.

My dad had taken me bowling for the first time and I have no recollection of my score or how well I threw the ball. My memory was of the way the fallen pins were automatically scooped away and new pins were inserted by a machine. I was fascinated every time I watched it and was determined to build one as soon as I got home.

The minute we got back in the house, I ran down the stairs to the basement and began working on my latest (and surely to be greatest) project. I had the basic equipment, a set of plastic bowling pins and a plastic bowling ball. Now all I needed to do was figure out a way of automatically setting them back up after they had been knocked down, just like at the bowling alley. After several hours trying everything I could think of, I had to call on my sister for help. This was going to have to be a two-person project.

However, despite both our efforts using everything we could find, including nails, glue, string and tape, I finally had to resort to the only thing I could think of.

I called my parents downstairs and told them it was finished. The pins were set up, and the ball was positioned on a plastic rail that sort of resembled the way it looked at the bowling alley. To the right of the pins was a large cardboard box with a small hole in it. I told my dad to go ahead and throw the ball. After knocking down all the pins, an arm reached out of the hole in the cardboard box and set them back up.

At first there was silence on the part of my parents. But then they could no longer contain themselves. I recall seeing tears running down my dad's face for the first time in my life. My mom, who always tried to be serious and encourage my projects, had to run up the stairs, quickly followed by my dad. I could hear them breaking out into uncontrollable laughter from the kitchen. At first I was disappointed, but then I figured I might as well laugh about it too. I had to admit the sight of seeing that arm come out of the box must have looked pretty funny.

After a few minutes, I lifted the cardboard box to let my sister out. She was covered in sweat after having been enclosed for the better part of an hour.

"Do we have to keep doing this?" she said, not looking too happy.

"No, I guess we're done," I replied.

"Good," she said. "I'm going to bed."

I followed her up the stairs a few minutes later, shutting off the lights to another in the long list of failed projects. It was to be the last one I ever remember attempting.

Chapter 2

~

We moved from Clinton to Bettendorf, another small town in Iowa, when I was nine and about to enter the third grade. I didn't have to worry about taking the bus because we moved into a house only one block away from school, another Catholic facility called Lourdes Memorial. We also lived next a park, where I would spend many hours.

As I outgrew my Superman outfit, so did I outgrow my early childhood heroes. Fictional characters were replaced by real-life ones, like Daniel Boone, Wyatt Earp, Jesse James, Wild Bill Hickok, Jim Bowie, and of course the legendary Davy Crockett.

I owned a coonskin cap, as did most of my friends, and followed Fess Parker as Davy every time he appeared on the TV screen. My favorite of his adventures was the Alamo, which I probably saw a dozen times. Although Davy and Jim and Colonel Travis all met their doom, they went down fighting against impossible odds. I was fascinated by that story, and played Davy to the hilt, swinging my musket when I ran out of ammunition against the never ending waves of Mexican soldiers.

As I began to read I started with the Classics Illustrateds, and then graduated to the Landmark books. I was partial toward stories about American history and historical figures. I especially enjoyed books about battles and war, from the American Revolution to the Civil War, to the two World Wars.

I had many heroes in those days but only one that I truly idolized. That was Abraham Lincoln. I don't recall the first time I heard or read about him, but once I did I couldn't get enough. I went to the library and read every book I could find on his life. My favorite movie was *Young Mr. Lincoln,* with Henry Fonda portraying the man I so admired. And I watched in awe a TV special called *Meet Mr. Lincoln*, which told of his life in words and pictures. They sold a record and book from the show that my parents later bought for me. I played it so many times I had every word memorized.

My biggest thrill was the trip my dad took us on to visit the places where Lincoln grew up and lived. I remember walking through the log cabin in New Salem, Illinois, where he grew up, and then visiting his home in Springfield where he spent his days as a lawyer. I remember actually getting to touch the desk and chair where he spent his time reading and working. Eventually, like all my other heroes, he would fade into memory. But for those years growing up I don't recall admiring anyone in history more than Honest Abe Lincoln.

My mom and dad were heroes to me in those days too. I had fond memories of my childhood, due in large part to them. They basically just let me be me. They went along with me playing out my boyhood heroes and encouraged me during my many failed experiments, even though they knew I had no chance of succeeding. I will always remember that of them.

One of the other things I will always remember was my mom's cooking. She once read in a magazine that eating meat that wasn't fully cooked could give you tapeworms. So she overcooked everything so much that it was difficult cutting and even tougher chewing. We had two choices of how we wanted our meat prepared, overdone or burnt. The magazine article apparently listed undercooked pork as the most dangerous for getting tape worms, and the end result were pork chops that were like eating a catcher's mitt with sauce on it.

My two best friends during my early days in Bettendorf were Barry Owens and Karl Rhomberg, who lived in my neighborhood and were in my class at school. We hung around almost every day together, at the park or riding our bikes around town.

Bikes to a kid our age were as essential as a truck to a delivery driver. It got us to where we were going, which was usually nowhere in particular. Unless it was snowing or pouring rain, my buddies and I were on our bikes, usually from morning until dusk. In those days kids were allowed to go off on their own without their parents worrying about their whereabouts every five minutes. We would usually head out in the morning, stop at one of our friends' houses when we got hungry, and have his mother fix us lunch to tide us over for the rest of the day, before heading off again. As long as we were home in time for dinner everything was fine. It was a safer time back then. A trusting time. The bad guys were only on TV or in movies, not in real life, at least not in small towns in Iowa.

And there was my dog, Pokey, a loveable Beagle who started out as a cute little pup when we got him, but eventually grew into a portly dog with a stomach so large it made his legs look unusually tiny. When Pokey would walk through a puddle, there were five things that got wet, his four paws and the bottom of his stomach. No one in the family was quite sure how he became so fat but it may have had something to do with the fact that every time one of us saw that his bowl was empty we filled it with dog food, which he ate immediately, leaving it empty again and waiting for the next person to come along and say, "Oh, you poor dog, you must be hungry" and fill it up again.

But despite the fact that Pokey's day consisted mostly of eating and sleeping, he provided me with something that only dogs could give—, unconditional love. He was always at my side it seemed, lying next to me as I sat in a chair and watched TV, and sleeping at the foot of my bed at night until he became too old and heavy to make the jump, and would have to settle for lying on the floor next to me.

Then there was the opposite extreme,—my sister's cat, Pixie, whom I hated. She would scratch and claw you for no apparent reason, and worse, would do the same to Pokey even when he was harmlessly minding his own business.

Since Pokey wouldn't so much as harm a fly and never retaliate against Pixie, I took it upon myself to get even.

I would place the cat behind the corner drawer in my room so she couldn't get out, or set her on top of a door ledge and leave her there for hours until my sister noticed and screamed at me to get her down.

But whenever I was really upset with the cat my favorite way of getting even was to stuff her in a Lincoln Log can, tape the lid shut and roll her the down the stairs. Upon opening the can she would stumble around the room for several minutes and fall over as if drunk. It wasn't that I was a mean spirited kid who enjoyed torturing animals. I just couldn't stand the cat from hell and felt it was my obligation to teach it a lesson in humility. Despite my tormenting, Pixie didn't die of a heart attack and lived to a ripe old age before passing on, as did Pokey, my beloved dog and friend.

My dad was a big sports fan in those days and tried his best to get me interested too. His two favorite teams were the Chicago Cubs and the Iowa Hawkeyes, and he tried to pass the legacy on to me. We would listen to the Cubs and Iowa football games on the radio. I remember him jumping up and down and screaming whenever one of his teams did something good, while I sat there pretending to get excited along with him, but in reality not old enough yet to understand what the excitement was all about.

He decided the best way to spark my interest would be to take me to see a live game. Our first few experiences were something less than I am sure he had hoped for.

We went on a family trip to Chicago one summer in the late '50s, and he took me to Wrigley Field to watch a Cubs game. I have no recollection who they played or what the score was or even if they won. My excitement came from the fact that people actually walked through the stands and handed out food and beverages to the fans. I couldn't believe it. Soon I was sitting there with a hot dog, Coke, popcorn, and a frosty malt on my lap. I was in heaven. But before I could barely enjoy my first bite my dad leaped from his chair screaming and spilling my food off my lap and onto the floor.

"Look what you did, dad," I said, totally stunned.

"Who cares?" he replied. "Ernie just hit a home run."

"Ernie who?" I said, caring only about the feast I was about to engulf that had now become garbage.

"Ernie who?" he replied, as if he couldn't believe I didn't know. "Ernie Banks, that's who." And so I sat and sulked through the rest of the game, blaming my delirious dad for ruining my day.

That fall we tried again by heading up to Iowa City for a Hawkeye game. On the trip up my dad kept telling me how great the Hawks were and that they had been to two Rose Bowls over the past three years.

I barely remember watching those games on TV, and my dad screaming and yelling as always whenever Iowa did something good, while I tried my best to join him in his excitement.

We entered the stadium on a crisp fall afternoon and my first reaction was how big the place seemed and how many people there were. I asked him who they were playing, and he said, "TCU. Don't worry, they aren't very good. The Hawks will kill them."

I thought how odd that expression seemed. "Kill them?" I recall thinking. My guess was that meant Iowa was supposed to win the game, but what a strange way to put it. "Killing" happened in the wars and battles I read about in the history books, not in football games. The Hawks did indeed "kill" TCU as my dad predicted. And as we headed out of the stadium he asked if I enjoyed the game.

"Sure, I guess," I shrugged.

"Pick out something," he said, as we passed a souvenir stand. "Anything you want."

After looking around for a few minutes, I said "I'll take a TCU pennant." The look on my dad's face was as if someone had died.

"A TCU pennant? No, you don't want a TCU pennant," he said. "There's Iowa pennants and hats and shirts and sweaters. You can pick out any one of those you want."

I certainly didn't intend to hurt my dad's feelings but for some reason I insisted on the TCU pennant.

Obviously heartbroken, my dad finally said to the vendor, "One TCU pennant please."

But there were no hard feelings afterward. I remember my dad and I going to a local sports store a few days later and buying both an Iowa and Cubs pennant and pinning them on my wall along side the infamous TCU one. I was slowly but surely becoming the sports fan my dad hoped I would be.

However, there was to be another team that would soon enter the picture. My grandparents had taken me with them on vacation out East that following summer, and along the way we stopped in South Bend, Indiana. We managed to get inside Notre Dame Stadium where my grandfather took my picture standing on the field. (I still have it to this day). "Cherish this moment, son," he said. "You're standing on hallowed ground."

I wasn't sure what he meant by that but judging by the tone of his voice it must have been something pretty important. As we walked through the campus I asked him what was so special about this place.

"A lot of famous people walked these grounds that you are standing on," he said. "Knute Rockne, George Gipp, the Four Horsemen." Although I had never heard of those names, the way he said it with the seriousness in his voice made me realize they must be special people. As he pointed out all of the famous landmarks on the campus I became more and more impressed.

"Were they famous men like Abraham Lincoln?" I asked.

"Well maybe not the same as Abraham Lincoln, but they were famous in their own way," he responded. "They were famous athletes."

I continued to question him, growing more and more curious. "What made them so famous?" I said.

"They helped take a tiny Catholic school and build a football team that not only competed against much larger schools but often beat them. They have even been voted the best football team in the country several times."

The more my grandfather talked the more impressed I became. It was like David beating Goliath, (one of my favorite bible stories), to hear the way he told it. Of all my boyhood heroes none of them had ever been sports figures, up until now. That day turned out to be the highlight of my trip, and would turn me into a Notre Dame fan for life.

As soon as I got back home from the trip I told my dad all about our adventure to South Bend and about the stories my grandfather told me. I asked him if we could buy a Notre Dame pennant.

"Notre Dame?" he said, unimpressed. "You really like them that much? They're boring. They win all the time. You don't like them as much as Iowa, do you?"

After giving it some thought, all I could think to say was, "I like them better than TCU."

That brought a smile to his face, and soon after I had my Notre Dame pennant pinned on my wall next to the others.

My dad was also a hunter and a fisherman, but failed to get me interested in either sport. My one and only fishing adventure with my dad was spending eight hours in a boat in the middle of a lake one day without catching one fish. And our first hunting experience together turned out to be our last when I followed my dad through the woods hunting animals, me with a BB gun and him with a twelve gauge shotgun. I begged him to let me shoot at something with his gun, and after spotting a rabbit cowering in a corner of a field he handed me the gun.

"OK, go for it," he said. "But remember two things. First, it will kick back on you when you fire so hold your shoulder tight, and second, aim at it's head or tail."

I aimed and shot, and hit the rabbit square in the middle, obliterating it into a hundred pieces. Sick to my stomach, I handed the gun back to my dad, and never went hunting again the rest of my life.

Chapter 3

~

As I grew from childhood to adolescence, so grew my love for sports. My dad had succeeded in turning me into a Cubs fan, and I listened to every game I could on WGN. And we watched football games every Saturday on TV while listening to the Hawks on the radio. Back then there weren't the wall-to-wall games from morning until night like today. We had only three channels to choose from, CBS, NBC and ABC, and were lucky to get maybe one or two games a week. And I was soon to discover another team to add to my collection of favorites, a team who played their games on Sundays,—The Chicago Bears. They were on TV every week, and played a different brand of football than the college guys. The Bears didn't just block or tackle their opponents, they mauled them. They were mean, tough, and scary. They even had a nickname that fit them perfectly,— "The Monsters of the Midway."

Soon I was no longer content just watching games. I wanted to play them as well. My dad spent many hours with me in the back yard and the park next door which had a ball diamond and a basketball court. He taught me how to hit, catch, and throw a baseball, dribble and shoot a basketball, and toss and catch a football.

I tried out for Little League and got on a team. My claim to fame was hitting a home run in my first official at bat, and making the all-star team as a third baseman by my second year.

I also made it as a starter on our grade school basketball team and as a wide receiver on the flag football team. I was tall and skinny as a rail, with arms and legs that resembled broom handles. But I was a decent athlete and competitive in every sport I played.

There was one thing I wasn't competitive or interested in during my grade school days. That was fighting. I got along with most of my classmates and had my share of friends, but unfortunately the designated class bully had it in for me for some reason and constantly harassed me. His name was Jimmy Beaman, (who would later gain fame as the main subject of a book called *The Rooms of Heaven*). He was shorter than me, but stocky and talked tough. He tormented those he knew he could intimidate, and I was among them. A week didn't go by that he didn't want to challenge me to a fight. I didn't want to fight him, or anybody for that matter. But inevitably the showdown would come.

We were in my back yard one day playing ball with a bunch of guys and Jimmy didn't like something I did or said and, as usual, challenged me to a fight. But this time was different. Instead of just talking, he actually started swinging at me. "Hit him back," the others yelled. And finally I did. I then ran into the house, crying.

My parents had been watching the whole thing out the window and when they asked me if I was hurt I said no.

"Then what's the matter?" they asked.

"Because I didn't want to hit him," I said, and went up to my room. As much as I hated that day and that moment, it was the last time he ever confronted me. Like most bullies, Jimmy liked doing the hitting but didn't like getting hit back.

I broke my nose twice, but neither time was the result of a fight. The first time I was teasing my grandparents dog, Tippy, by holding a piece of candy just out of his reach and pulling it back each time he lunged for it. After several attempts, he decided my nose would be just as good as the candy and clamped onto it and wouldn't let go. Eventually my parents heard me screaming and pried him off me and took me to the hospital where I got stitched up.

The second time came when I was attempting to pitch in a pick up game at the park with a bunch of guys I didn't know too well. I started from the pitcher's mound, but kept coming up short on my pitches, and finally the batter, (whose name I cannot recall, only the fact that he was bigger than me), told me to move up closer, which I did. I kept moving up until I finally got one over the plate. Unfortunately he proceeded to hit a line drive right back at me, striking me directly on the nose, knocking me down and out. When I came to he was standing over me, watching in horror as the blood poured all over my face, and said, "I'll be out, OK?" as if that would make everything better. Once again I was on my way to the hospital and once again having my nose patched up.

Going to a Catholic school meant being taught by nuns and priests. And we were scared to death of them. Nuns excelled in two things, teaching and discipline, and not necessarily in that order. I'm sure there were some nice nuns somewhere, they just weren't at our school. They were for the most part mean spirited, and demanded respect at all times. And when they didn't get it, they punished the guilty party.

There were no rules back then regarding teachers physically punishing their students. They had free reign and they used it. A slap to the back of the head or a ruler to the knuckles was commonplace to those who misbehaved.

And the worst thing a kid could say to a nun was to address her as "stir," as in, "Yes, stir, I promise never to do that again."

"I am not a 'stir,' I am a sister," she would always come back with. "You will address me that way."

Actually "stir" was rather appropriate, I thought, considering we didn't regard them as women, but rather as authority figures. It was kind of a cross between "sister" and "sir." They just never saw it that way. They figured we were either being lazy or insulting.

I never had a priest as a teacher while at Lourdes but they were always around, and we knew it. If nuns were the cops, then priests were the Gestapo. If you were ever sent to a priest by a nun for disciplinary reasons you were in serious trouble.

I had to mainly deal with priests while serving my tenure as an altar boy. When you became old enough you didn't volunteer, you were pressed into service, sort of like military duty. We even had to wear uniforms, which consisted of a long black robe called a "cassock" and a white outer garment called a "surplice." In those days the mass was said in Latin, which meant we had to memorize prayers in a foreign language. There was no "In the name of the Father, Son and Holy Spirit" back then. It was "In nomine Patris, et Filii, et Spiritus Sancti."

There were two incidents that I remember from my altar boy days. One was spilling hot wax all over my hand and arm when attempting to tilt the candle in order to light it before mass. The other was a rather bizarre ritual that altar boys had to go through during the Easter Vigil season, which was to kneel for long hours at a time on the altar, often at odd hours of the night. We worked in shifts so that there was at least one altar boy on duty at all time. There aren't too many things more boring or hard on the knees that having to kneel for four hours at two o'clock in the morning.

There were two aromas that were always prevalent at school,—vomit and dog poop. It seemed like someone threw up almost every day, and the janitor would apply that sawdust stuff that dried up the mess but still left the stench. And it was a given that some person would have dog poop on their shoes and drag it with them into the classroom. There was a particular odor to dog poop that was different from a fart, which was the third most prevalent odor in school.

Winters in Iowa usually sucked. We couldn't ride our bikes or play in the park, or go outside for recess. But they did provide a reward every now and then. They were called "snow days." I would often look out my window during the night and at the first sight of snowflakes falling I would immediately turn on the radio, hoping to hear those glorious words, "School has been cancelled tomorrow due to an impending snowstorm." One day it was so cold the school furnace could not keep up and we were all sent home. Of course we didn't go home. Despite the fact that it was something like 20 degrees below zero we looked upon it as a day off school and spent the rest of the day playing in the snow. When my mom and dad found out that they let us out of school and didn't let the parents know, they were furious. After checking me for frostbite and telling me to take a hot bath I realized I wasn't in any trouble. It was the school they were mad at, not me.

In sixth grade I met a new kid named Mike McCarthy, who had transferred from another school. We soon became best friends. He was carefree and totally without fear, and dared us to take chances and risks we would never have taken on our own. He once talked three of us into getting on his bike and going down a steep hill which led to the school. We all hopped on and headed down the hill, going faster with each passing second. I was on the handle bars and told him to slow down. "I can't," he replied, "I don't have any brakes." That was Mike McCarthy.

Weekends were something you lived for during the school year, starting on Monday morning. But I hated Sundays, which limited my weekends to Friday night and Saturday. For me the weekend ended when **Chiller Theater**, (later to be renamed **Creature Features**), was over. **Chiller Theater** was a double feature of horror movies ranging from the likes of **Frankenstein Meets the Wolf Man** to **Creature From The Black Lagoon** that began after the 10 o'clock news on Saturday night and lasted until the wee hours of the morning. My mom would tell me I could only watch one movie and I would reply, "OK, I'll watch the second one." Actually that probably only happened once but I thought it was clever of me so I like to think that conversation took place each week.

Then came Sunday, which for most kids was a day off but

for me was a day of obligations. The routine was church in the morning, followed by driving to Clinton to spend the day visiting relatives, and finally returning home that evening and having to do my homework, which I always put off until the last minute.

My fondness for movies extended beyond *Chiller Theater*. I enjoyed watching them on TV, but especially loved going to the theater and getting to see them on the big screen. As much as I liked reading books about history and wars and battles it was nothing compared to watching the historical epics of the late '50s and early '60s, movies like *Ben-Hur, Spartacus, The Alamo, El Cid, The Longest Day, 55 Days At Peking*, and *Lawrence of Arabia*. And I loved the music almost as much as the movies themselves. While my friends were buying top 40 singles and Elvis albums I was buying movie soundtracks.

I probably saw *El Cid* a total of eight times while it was at the theater. My parents took me to see it for the first time and I fell in love with it. Charlton Heston being strapped to his horse after being mortally wounded by an arrow and leading his troops to victory was the greatest thing I had ever seen on a movie screen. I begged my parents to take me again. Reluctantly they sat through it again with me, dozing off during most of it while I sat wide eyed enjoying every minute and waiting for the triumphant climax. A third time was out of the question, so I had to start relying on my friends. At first my mom or dad would drive us to the theater and pick us up, but after a while I had to take the city bus in order to see it. Eventually, it left the theater, but fortunately I had the soundtrack album to listen to and play every scene over again in my head.

Then there were the drive-in theaters, which were very popular in those days, but have become practically obsolete today. Instead of parking your car and walking into a theater you stayed in your car, placed a speaker in the window, and waited for it to get dark, at which point the movie would start. In the '50s and '60s drive-ins, at least in the Midwest, actually outnumbered movie theaters, which then consisted of separate buildings, showing one movie at each theater, as opposed to the super cinemas of today.

The first fast food restaurant to hit town was a McDonald's in the early '60s, and it would change the course of eating habits for thousands of people, including me. The first one I remember was a tiny building with a window that you walked up to and ordered your food. You could get a hamburger for 15 cents, fries for a dime, and a drink for a nickle, all in a matter of seconds. It would turn me into a fast food junkie to this day. Eventually, more McDonald's started sprouting up all over town, along with places like Sandy's and Henry's. Now of course, fast food restaurants are everywhere, and have evolved to where you can either dine in or drive through and pick up your food to go. A far cry from that first little building on Brady Street in Davenport.

I graduated from eighth grade in the spring of 1963. The question of what high school to go to came down to the public school in Bettendorf or the Catholic school in Davenport, a neighboring city. I had had my fill of nuns and priests after eight years, but my parents insisted on me continuing with my Catholic education.

Chapter 4

~

I began my freshman year at Assumption High School in fall of 1964. I started out as a shy kid, and with the exception of knowing a handful of friends from Lourdes, felt overwhelmed among all the unfamiliar faces, especially the girls. And the school I attended didn't help. Technically it was a boys and girls school but for some reason they separated us during classes. The only time we boys ever saw girls was in the cafeteria at lunch. The term for it was "co-institutional." I guess the idea behind it was that we would concentrate more in class if we weren't distracted by staring at the opposite sex.

Needless to say, I didn't get too many opportunities to hang out with girls or ask them out on dates. But I did have a secret crush on one girl. "Secret" being the key word since I was too scared to even speak to her. Her name was Mary Lujack, daughter of the legendary Notre Dame quarterback and Heisman Trophy winner Johnny Lujack. We rode on the same school bus, and I tried to sit as close as possible to her every day. She never seemed to notice me, and I'm quite sure she had no idea I even existed.

Then came the day that I thought was going to change everything. She always got dropped off before me and on a particular Friday after school I noticed she left her school book on her seat. This was my chance. I picked up her book and called her house that night to tell her I would bring it over to her the next day. As I recall, her mom answered the phone and said thanks and that she would tell Mary.

I don't think I slept a wink that night. I just kept thinking of meeting Mary, asking her out, and with any luck getting to meet her father and seeing the Heisman Trophy. I jumped out of bed the next morning, showered, brushed my teeth three times, combed my hair, shaved what little stubble of facial hair I had, and wore my best outfit. My mom offered to drive me over to her house but I figured Mary would be more impressed if I walked the book over to her, especially considering it was a good three miles and snowing as well.

I fantasized the entire trip over that Mary would greet me at the door, thank me for returning her book, and invite me in to meet her dad, who would shake my hand, spend hours telling me stories of his days at Notre Dame, as I held the famed Heisman Trophy in my hands. They would invite me to stay for lunch, and I would end up asking Mary to go to the movies with me, which of course she would gladly say yes to.

When I finally arrived and rang the doorbell, it wasn't Mary who opened the door, but rather her little brother. When I told him who I was and that I had Mary's book he said, "I'll give it to her," and slammed the door in my face. I stood there motionless for several minutes, not believing what had just happened. My hopes and dreams shattered, I finally turned to make the trip back home. It was the longest three miles I can ever remember.

I never got the opportunity or courage to talk to her again.

As I neared my 16th birthday, my biggest excitement was the anticipation of getting my driver's license and trading in my bike for a car. Back then there was no such thing as driver's education. My dad taught me how to drive, and obtaining a license was a simple matter of passing a written exam and a driver's test. I passed the written part, and all I had to do was drive the family car along with a police officer around town while my dad waited back at the license bureau.

I was doing fine through most of the test, driving as carefully and slowly as I could. Then came the infamous right hand turn that would change everything. We were driving along a two-lane road in town when the officer instructed me to take a right turn onto a busy four lane street. There was a single turning lane which was separated by a median. When I went to make the turn the light was green, and I proceeded slowly through the median and onto the main street. Suddenly the officer shouted, "Stop!" I slammed on the brakes and pulled over to the curb as hordes of onrushing cars zoomed past us.

"Sorry to yell at you, but I thought we were going to get hit," he said. "You may proceed now." Apparently the timing of the stop light was such that by the time I had driven through the right-hand turn lane, the light had changed.

When we got back to the license bureau I remember seeing my dad standing there, smiling proudly.

"Well, how did it go?" he said confidently.

"I'm sorry to inform you of this, sir," replied the stern

police officer. "Not only did your son fail the test but I am going to have to issue a citation for running a red light."

My dad's smile quickly turned into a disheartened frown. He didn't say a word.

"The citation must be paid within seven days and the driving test can be retaken within two weeks," said the officer, while writing out the ticket and handing it to my dad. Needless to say, the trip home was not a pleasant one. My plan was to drive my dad home with my new license. Instead, I sat in the passenger seat while he drove, not saying a word. I could always tell my dad was upset when he didn't talk.

The two weeks slowly passed and I tried it again, this time passing the test with flying colors. I was officially the proud owner of a driver's license. I couldn't wait to get behind the wheel on my own and show off in front of my envious friends who had not yet gotten their license. I begged my parents to let me take the car out for "a spin" that first night. They grudgingly agreed, but lectured me for what seemed like an hour and gave me a strict set of rules, which of course I forgot by the time I pulled out of the driveway.

I picked up my friend Karl and planned on picking up Barry until Karl told me he was out on a date and planning to make out with the girl at Duck Creek Park.

"Let's drive through there and see if we can find them," said Karl.

"Barry's going out with a girl?" I said. "No way. Who is she?" He couldn't remember her name but swore that it was true. I wasn't buying it but he talked me into driving through the park none the less.

Unfortunately, it was past the park's closing hours and a policeman was pulling cars over to issue tickets.

As we drove near him he signaled for us to pull over along the side of the road. After sitting there for a few minutes as he was writing out a ticket for someone else, Karl said to me, "Just take off. By the time the cop runs back to his car we'll be long gone."

"You're kidding, right?" I said. "I'm not taking off." But he kept insisting that we could get away with it and the thought did enter my mind that the last thing I needed was to have to hand over another traffic ticket to my dad. He would never let me use the car again. So I went for it. I put the car in gear and floored the accelerator, praying to God that Karl's plan would work.

The park road was horseshoe like, so all we needed to do to get away was follow the road around the bend and back around to the main street. Unfortunately, I had hit the accelerator so hard that it stuck to the floor, sending us flying around the bend like a bat out of hell.

"I think you can slow down now," said Karl. "I don't see him following us."

"I can't slow down," I screamed. "The damn gas pedal is stuck. Do something."

Karl tried in vain to pull up on it with his hands while I kept pushing on it with my foot to try and loosen it. I didn't want to put the car in neutral or turn off the ignition for fear that the police were coming after us.

We were getting closer and closer to the main street, and still were unable to free the pedal. The only thing I could think to do was put my foot on the brake to at least slow us down. Tires squealing as we neared the intersection and still going at least 50 miles an hour, I started honking the horn to warn drivers on the main street that we weren't about to stop at the stop sign and were going through the intersection no matter what.

Thanks to the grace of God, we made it across without getting hit. After crossing the street I finally put the car in neutral and pulled over into an alley. After several minutes we were finally able to get the accelerator unstuck. We waited until we were sure the police weren't still looking for us before starting the car and heading back home.

"Great idea, Karl." I said sarcastically. "Remind me never to listen to you again."

"Hey, I didn't know your damn accelerator was going to get stuck," he said. "Don't blame me. We didn't getting a ticket, did we? You should be thanking me."

All I cared about was getting back home and forgetting what had just happened. After dropping off Karl and walking into the house my parents asked me how it went.

"Fine," I said. "I think I'll head upstairs to bed. Goodnight." I never did tell them how close my first night out with the car came to being my last.

The remainder of my high school years weren't quite as memorable as that night. I didn't study very hard or earn that good of grades, just enough to get by, and other than American history I wasn't interested in any particular subjects. I went on a few dates, but didn't party much or get involved in beer drinking like a lot of my classmates. As for sports, I tried out for the football team but was too tall and lanky to be considered dangerous to any opponent. Even though I had good hands as a receiver, I mainly sat on the bench. I never tried out for the baseball team, figuring I was probably most suited to play basketball, considering the body God had given me.

My dad had constructed a hoop in our driveway and I practiced every day, hoping to make the freshman team, which I did, although I played very little that year and ended up making a decision that I would always regret. I decided to quit the team during the season out of frustration and never went back my sophomore or junior years. I loved the game and continued to play with my friends in pickup games and in intramurals at school. I also continued to grow, both in height and bulk, and got better as time went on.

"Man, you should have stuck it out your freshman year," a friend would say to me after a pickup game. "You're better than half the guys on the varsity team."

I spent my sophomore and junior years writing about sports instead of playing them. I was the sports editor for the school newspaper and went to basketball games and interviewed the players who I wished were my teammates.

Fortunately, someone else besides my friends noticed an improvement in my game too. After watching intramurals during gym class, the head varsity coach stopped over to talk to me and invited me to try out for the team my senior year. I was ecstatic. I thought I had lost my chance of ever playing high school basketball and now I was getting a second opportunity.

It was tough at the beginning. Most of the players were back from their junior season and the starting lineup was pretty much set. I was the outsider, trying my best to become a part of the team but feeling like my teammates didn't need or want me around, that they would be fine without me. I spent most of the first half of the season on the bench, and only got to play a few minutes now and then to relieve the starters. But then following a good week of practice and playing as hard as I could, I was told by the coach just before the game on Friday that I was going to start at center. Needless to say, I was surprised, as were the other starters, especially the guy whose place I was taking.

I played well that night, blocking shots, getting my share of rebounds and scoring some points. My teammates rarely threw me the ball, so most of my points came on offensive rebounds and tip-ins off missed shots. It wasn't that my teammates resented me, they just didn't trust me or feel like I was one of them yet. That wasn't the case with the center who had lost his starting position to me. He was mad and pounded me hard in practices the rest of the year, trying to get his starting job back. But I held my own and remained the starter the rest of the year.

I'll always remember what my coach had to say about me at the awards banquet after the season as he talked about the departing seniors. "Pat Triplett led us in rebounds, blocked shots and field goal percentage. I just wish he would have shot more."

So did I. I just never got the opportunity. I never felt like I was part of the offense, even though we had set plays with me getting the ball during practices. I didn't harbor any grudges against my teammates. I just felt fortunate to be a part of the team. The only thing I regretted was having quit my freshman year and wondering how good I could have been had I stayed and played all four years. Maybe good enough to earn a college scholarship and keep playing ball somewhere. But because of my decision, I'll never know what might have been.

Chapter 5

~

My high school days were behind me, having done the cap and gown ceremony and receiving my diploma, and more importantly, coming out of my shell. During the summer of 1967 I was to discover girls, poker, and beer. And that summer would end by embarking on one of the most memorable journeys of my life.

We had become a two-car family, and even though my mom worked part-time, I pretty much had access to a car whenever I wanted it. I dated a girl the better part of the summer. I got a job at Alcoa in Bettendorf, where my dad worked, and spent many nights playing poker with the guys, and enjoying a newly discovered beverage. Although we were underage, we always seemed to find ways of getting beer, whether it was an older brother, a friend of a friend, or a grocery store or liquor shop that didn't ask for an ID. The toughest part was sneaking it into the house and into the basement, hoping our parents didn't catch us. The best nights were the ones when someone's parents would be gone and we had free reign of the house. Other times we just took it to a park and drank while telling jokes and stories.

I still lived at home, but the days of sitting around watching TV or playing board games with my sister, or cards with the family after dinner were fast becoming a thing of the past. I was becoming a typical 18 year old, looking to party and just have fun.

Fortunately, I never got into smoking cigarettes or doing marijuana. And I have my friend Karl to thank for that. He got a hold of a pack of cigarettes one day and passed them around for us to try. I tried puffing on one a few times but then he said, "No, you're doing it all wrong. In order to get the full effect you have to inhale it and then let it out slowly." After trying it a couple of times, it made me sick. I never wanted to smoke a cigarette again, legally or otherwise, and never did.

Midway through the summer the subject of college came up, and my parents took me to several schools to see where I wanted to go and what I wanted to study. We visited mostly local and in-state schools. I think they wanted me to continue to pursue a Catholic education, and my choices eventually were narrowed down to St. Ambrose, the local school in Davenport, and Loras College in Dubuque, which was about an hour's drive away. I chose Loras. It wasn't that I didn't enjoy my family or that I was unhappy living at home, but the thought of being on my own and gaining my independence was a big part of what led to my decision.

In late August, two of my friends, Mike McCarthy and Roger Mohr, had come up with this idea of heading out to Colorado for a week for one last fling before we all headed off for college, and asked me to join them.

"Why Colorado?" I said.

"Because they have mountains and you can drink legally there," was their response.

"Drink legally? Really?" I said, totally ignoring the part about the mountains. "Count me in."

But there were many obstacles to overcome before such a trip could become a reality. None of us owned our own car, and asking to borrow one of our parents cars would be out of the question. And I wasn't sure how Mike's and Roger's parents felt about the idea, but I knew talking mine into it wasn't going to be easy. And lastly, there was the money part. I had saved up some cash over the summer but it was supposed to go toward college. And even with that, it wouldn't come close to covering the cost of a trip like this one. I knew it was going to be a tough sell, but I dug in my heels one evening after dinner and brought it up to my parents.

"There's no way in the world we would let you do something like that," was their first reaction. "Besides, Mike and Roger's parents would never go for it either." I had my work cut out for me. But I continued to press on, only to hear one reason after another why I couldn't go. My dad took the more practical approach, while my mom was more on the emotional side.

"You have no way of getting there and no money," was my dad's angle.

"I have some money saved from working this summer," I replied.

"That is supposed to help pay for college," he came back with.

And then my mom kicked in with, "Colorado is such a long way away and you're just kids. You wouldn't have any idea where you were going or how to get there. And it would be dangerous driving through all those mountains. And you don't know anybody out there that you could stay with or call for help if you got in trouble."

The next day Mike and Roger called me. "Well, are you going or not?"

"It's not looking too good at this point," I replied. "Are your parents letting you go?" They both said yes.

"Plus," they said, "There's an ad this guy put in the paper that says he has a truck that we could rent for the week. We're set to go, man."

That gave me an idea. "I'll ask my parents to call yours and they can say it's OK with them that you guys can go. Maybe they can talk mine into it."

After talking on the phone at length with their parents that night my dad began to cave. "You're still going to need money," he said. "Even if you use what you've saved up, it won't be enough."

"Maybe you and mom could give me some as a going away present for college or an early birthday gift," I said.

"Maybe," he replied. I was making progress. But there was still my mom to convince, which wasn't going to be easy considering she got teary-eyed every time I brought up the subject.

"I don't want you to go," she pleaded with me. "I know something bad will happen to you out there. Please say you won't go."

"I'll be fine, mom, I swear. I'm not a kid anymore. I can take care of myself. And it's not like I'm going alone. There will be three of us to watch each other and make sure nothing bad happens. It's only for a week. We'll be fine. I promise." I used up all the ammunition I had left. Now all I could do was hope.

Reluctantly, my parents finally agreed to let me go. I had done it. The next day we rented the truck from the guy, and he also agreed to let us mount a camper in the bed, which we also rented. Now we not only had a vehicle but a place to sleep at night as well to save having to spend money on motel rooms. Things were looking up.

At last the big day arrived. We packed everything we could think of in the camper and were ready to head west. My mom gave me the biggest hug she ever gave me in her life, and had that look on her face like it would be the last time she would ever see me again, then ran into the house.

"It's going to be a long week around here," said my dad. "I don't suppose there's any chance of you changing your mind, is there?" He knew what my answer would be. So he shook my hand, gave me some spending money, and told me to be careful and call whenever we could to let them know we were OK.

"Thanks, dad," I said. "See you in a week," and off we went.

We made it as far as Nebraska the first day, and decided to pull off the interstate because of bad weather and spend the night. In fact, the local radio station we were listening to had issued a tornado warning for the area. As we slept in the camper, we were awakened by a loud sound that kept getting louder.

"Is it a tornado?" I asked.

"No," said either Mike or Roger. "It sounds more like a train." We stared at each other for a moment and then jumped out of our beds, Roger and I heading for the door while Mike grabbed the keys and started up the truck. We looked out to see a freight train heading very quickly in our direction, then looked down at the ground to notice we had virtually parked right along side the train track.

"Hurry Mike, get us the hell out of here," we yelled. He managed to move the truck in time as the train sped by us.

After collecting our breaths Roger said, "The next time we decide to spend the night somewhere let's check to make sure we don't park on a damn train track." We all made a mental note of that.

The next morning the weather cleared and we were on our way again. The drive through Nebraska was boring, even more so than Iowa. It was flat and had nothing scenic about it unless you liked farms, cows, and endless pastures and fields. But later that afternoon toward sunset we noticed something different.

"What's that up ahead on the horizon?" one of us asked. As we drove closer we saw what it was. Mountains. "Mountains!" we screamed joyously. "We made it!"

Sure enough, the endless flatlands of Nebraska had turned into the scenic wonder of the Rocky Mountains. We had made it to Colorado. And our first stop was a little town called Julesburg, where we were to put the "legal drinking" thing to the test. We stopped at the first bar we saw and ordered three beers.

"I need to see some ID's guys," said the bartender. We nervously opened our wallets and showed him our driver's licenses, holding our breath. After checking them out he said the words we were hoping to hear. "What will it be, gentlemen, three Coors?" It was at that moment we knew we had arrived.

And our goal was to make the most of it. Fort Collins, Boulder, and Estes Park were our next destinations. The scenery was gorgeous and the beer was cold. Estes Park was one of our particular favorites, a party town, alive with young people like us just looking to have a good time. We could have spent the rest of the week there and been happy, but decided to move on the next morning to experience as much of Colorado as we could.

We headed though Rocky Mountain National Park with all it's twisting turns and scenic beauty, and even stopped along the way to climb some mountains. Eventually we reached the other side at a place called Grand Lake. After spending a few hours there I said I wanted to head back to Estes Park for the night. Mike and Roger were leery of having to navigate our way back through the mountains in the dark, especially after having spent most of the afternoon drinking beer. But I talked them into it and volunteered to drive.

"We'll be there in a few hours and we'll have a great time," I persuaded them. Roger got in on the passenger side and Mike laid down in the back seat.

But there was one thing we didn't anticipate as we headed back through the mountains. Because of the elevation, the clouds had descended below the mountain tops to the point where it was like driving through a dense fog. What made matters worse was that there were virtually no guard rails to protect us as we rounded the now treacherous bends in the road. I drove as slowly as possible, but soon it was becoming nearly impossible to see. Finally I stopped the truck and asked Roger to open the door to see how close to the edge of the road we were. His answer was not one that I wanted to hear.

"Stay right where you are and don't drive another foot," he said, his face looking pale.

"Why? Are we close to the edge?" I replied.

"We're not close to the edge. We're on the edge," he said. "When I stuck my foot out it didn't touch ground. Turn off the truck. We're spending the night right here."

"We can't park in the middle of the road," I said. "What if somebody hits us?"

"No one is going to be crazy enough to drive through this stuff," said Roger. "And even if they do, I would rather get hit from behind than drive off the cliff. But if it makes you feel any better turn on the emergency lights."

"What if the battery goes dead during the night?" I said.

"Better a dead battery than three dead people," Roger replied. "Let's just try and get some sleep and we'll get going first thing in the morning when this clears."

And so we left the truck sitting in the road and went to bed. Finally daylight came and the clouds lifted. We got out to see how close we were to the edge of the road. Roger was right. Had we proceeded a few more feet, we would have driven off the cliff, with nothing to stop us but 1,200 feet of air, followed by the ground.

"What's going on?" asked Mike, who had slept through

the entire ordeal. "Are we in Estes Park?"

"No, although we did almost visit the bottom of Rocky Mountain Park," I replied sarcastically.

We spent one more night in Estes Park and then headed for Denver the next day, phoning our parents to tell them we were fine and having a great time. We spent most of that day traveling around the Denver area before heading south. The next day we reached Colorado Springs. While driving around we noticed a place that rented motorcycles by the hour.

"Let's do it," said Mike. "It would be fun to ride through the mountains on motorcycles."

"I've never been on a motorcycle and have no idea how to drive one," I said.

"Neither do I," said Mike. "So what, we'll figure it out. How tough could it be? How about you, Roger, ever ridden a motorcycle?"

"Nope," he replied, not sure, like me, if this was such a good idea. But Mike talked us into it, and after showing the guy our driver's licenses we were handed the keys to three motorcycles. And not little ones like mopeds. These were the real thing. We had never heard of a place that rented motorcycles like that and to this day I've never heard of another one. I'm pretty sure because of insurance costs and lawsuits that they have become obsolete.

We had to admit to the guy that we had never driven a motorcycle before and needed instructions on how to operate one. I figured he would take the keys away from us after hearing that, but instead he took the time to show us how to start, drive and stop them. Soon we were driving motorcycles through the streets of downtown Colorado

Springs, weaving our way in and out of traffic and headed toward the Rocky Mountains.

We finally reached a place called "Garden of the Gods," which was mountainous and challenging, especially for three novices on motorcycles. But we had the time of our lives, racing along the dirt roads and through the mountains, often as fast as we could go. We even challenged each other to races to see who could reach the top of the mountain first. We spent the whole day driving until we were exhausted. We managed to survive unharmed, and returned the motorcycles intact.

We left Colorado Springs and continued south, stopping along the way at places like Pueblo and Canon City. We drove up Pikes Peak and walked across Royal Gorge Bridge, which was both magnificent and scary at the same time, considering we were peering down over the edge at a river that was 1,000 feet below us.

Unfortunately, the week was coming to an end and we needed to think about heading home. After one last night of partying we headed back to the camper to get some sleep before starting back. But Mike insisted he was OK to drive and for Roger and I to get some sleep and take over for him in a few hours. So Mike started up the truck, and Roger and I headed to the back of the camper and immediately fell asleep. Sometime during the night we were abruptly awakened by loud noises and the truck shaking back and forth. We yelled up front at Mike to ask what happened.

"Nothing," he said. "Go back to sleep." When we awoke the next morning, we were surprised that Mike was still driving and we had nearly reached the Iowa border.

"I'll take over now," said Roger. "By the way, what was all that commotion about last night? Did you hit a bad spot in the road or something?" Mike finally confessed that he fallen asleep at the wheel and veered off the interstate and into a field. We got outside to look at the condition of the truck and other than a few minor scrapes it appeared fine.

"Why didn't you wake us?" I said to Mike. "One of us could have taken over."

"Because after I woke up and realized what happened, I was so scared that I was wide awake, and figured I might as well keep going and let you guys sleep." All I could think was, thank God he veered right instead of left, and into a pasture instead of oncoming cars.

We arrived home the next day and back to everyone's relieved parents. I'm sure my mom spent half the week in church and the other half on her knees praying.

"See, I told you we'd make it," I said to her as she grabbed and hugged me.

It was one of the unforgettable experiences of my life, one that Mike and Roger and I still reminisce about to this day.

Chapter 6

~

Soon I was off again, this time to Dubuque and the start of my college career in the fall of 1967. And while the Colorado trip, especially those nights in Estes Park, provided me with a glimpse of what teenage party life was like, it was only an inkling of what was to come during my days at Loras. For those who never got the chance to experience dorm life in college, there is no way to fully explain it and do it justice. The best way I can think to describe it is a reference to a movie called *Windy City*. There was a scene where someone asked a serious, successful middle-aged businessman if he could be anything he wanted, what would it be. His response was, "I want to be a sophomore in college again."

So my parents and I loaded up the family Chevy and headed north. We unpacked my things in my dorm room, which I was to share with a street wise kid from Chicago named Eddie Quinn. When it became time for them to head back, predictably my mom became teary eyed and hugged me, while my dad shook my hand and wished me luck.

And then suddenly it hit me. There I was, on my own for the first time in my life and surrounded by guys my age who I assumed were as interested as me in having a good time.

"Want to head downtown tonight and hit the bars?" asked Eddie.

"What if they ask for ID's?" I replied.

"No problem," he said. I've got a fake one, and I'll make one for you. Give me your driver's license." I handed it to him and he proceeded to change the 1948 on my birth date to 1946.

"It's not my best work, but it should do the job," he said. "Let's go find out what night life in Dubuque is all about."

And so began my college career. Instead of spending my first night reading the brochures on where to go the next day to sign up for classes or even what classes I was going to take, I was sitting in a bar with 40 other guys my age drinking one beer after another.

My dad had sat down with me before we left for Dubuque and explained in lengthy detail how a checking account worked. I barely paid attention and just took the checkbook when he handed it over to me.

"Now remember," he said, "whenever you write out a check, make sure to write the amount in the balance book so you can keep track of how much you have remaining." My parents had put a couple hundred dollars in my account to last me the semester.

I signed up for classes the next day and wrote out a check to pay for my school books, forgetting of course to mark it down in the balance book. I was to write out a lot of checks over the next few weeks, mostly for beer and pizza. I was making the most of being on my own, partying almost every night and shutting off the alarm clock the following morning, often skipping classes and sleeping in until noon. Then one day came the phone call.

"The bank called us," said my dad, sounding upset. "They said your account was overdrawn. How could that be?"

"They must have made a mistake," I replied. "I still have plenty of checks left."

"It doesn't matter how many checks you have left," he said, his voice becoming more heated. "Haven't you been keeping track of the money in the balance book like we went over?"

"Well, not exactly," I replied timidly. "I just figured as long as I had checks left I was OK."

Now he was really angry. "How could you possibly think that? And how could you spend all that money already when it was supposed to last all semester?"

"Well, I had to spend a lot on books and things," I said, trying to squirm my way out of this any way I could. But I wasn't doing a very good job. And then came the ultimatum.

"From now on we will start sending you five dollars a week in the mail. That's all you get. No more checking accounts and no more writing checks," my dad said, and then hung up the phone.

"Five dollars a week?" I thought to myself. That was going to put a dent in the lifestyle I had become accustomed to over the past few weeks. I was spending more than that on a daily basis. How was I going to get by on five bucks a week?

Later that evening Eddie said a bunch of the guys were going over to East Dubuque, which was basically a two block stretch of bars, strip joints and pizza parlors across the river in Illinois that we occasionally frequented. It was sort of a miniature, poor man's version of Bourbon Street in New Orleans.

"I can't go," I said dejectedly. "I'm broke. My dad called today and read me the riot act and told me I had spent all my money in my checking account, and from now on they were going to send me five dollars a week for spending money."

"Five dollars a week?" replied Eddie. "You can't live on five bucks a week. That's just wrong, man."

"I know, but that's how it is. I guess I'll stay in tonight and do some studying."

"Studying?" responded Eddie. I haven't seen you open a book since we got here."

"Well, it's time I start. I'm sure I must have an exam or two coming up."

"Wow, this is really sad, man," said my roommate, shaking his head. "Well, enjoy your studying. I'll have one for you."

And so I began to learn that college life was not all fun and games. I actually woke up the next morning and attended my early class, Physical Science, located on the other side of campus. When the teacher took roll call and got to my name he was shocked when I responded, "Here."

"I figured you were out to set the all time record for missed classes," he said sarcastically.

I was to spend the remainder of the semester doing more studying and attending more classes. But when that precious five dollars appeared in my mail slot each week, I used it to party with my friends until it was gone. I wasn't about to give up on my social life entirely. Today, five bucks wouldn't buy you two bottles of beer. But back then, you could drink the cheap stuff on tap for 25 cents a glass. Unfortunately, my late surge wasn't enough to save my grades for the first semester. But I rationalized that I was just being a typical 19 old away from home for the first time, and not being told every night to do my homework, or when to go to bed, or get up in the morning and go to school.

I met a guy who lived in our dorm one day named Steve England, and as we were talking, I asked him where he was from. He could have said any town in the United States and I would have believed him. But when he said, "Bettendorf, Iowa," I just stared at him.

"No you're not," I said. "I'm from Bettendorf, and I know every kid my age in town and you aren't one of them." My first thought was that he was some Commie spy from Russia who randomly picked Bettendorf on a map as the place he told people he was from. I was seriously thinking of asking him the question I once saw in a movie that you are supposed to ask suspected spies, which is how many homers Babe Ruth hit. But before I could say anything, Steve responded.

"Actually, I just moved to Bettendorf from Springfield, Illinois last week. I should have said I was from there instead. Sorry to confuse you. What a coincidence, huh?"

We both laughed and immediately became best friends.

I began to learn that not having much spending money anymore wasn't the worst thing in the world. There were plenty of moments when living in a dorm was fun without having to go downtown or order out for pizzas. I started eating in the school cafeteria, which was prepaid for as part of my tuition expenses. I remember one night asking Steve if he knew what they were having for dinner.

"Pork chops," he said, excitedly.

"Oh God, not pork chops," I responded. "I hate pork chops." But being broke, I decided to give them a try. To my surprise they were delicious. I couldn't believe something that I dreaded so much growing up could taste so good. And steak night became my favorite, discovering what a medium rare piece of beef tasted like.

And there were the pranks we in the dorm would pull on the serious students who were more interested in studying and getting good grades than hanging with us and having fun. In other words, the dorm geeks. Some of our personal favorites were "pennying" them in their rooms. "Pennying" consisted of leaning against their door from the outside and wedging three or four pennies between the door and the frame, making it impossible for them to get out. The best time to do it was during the night or early in the morning when we knew they had classes to attend. Our mischievous plan would cause them to have to bang on the door until someone let them out, usually one of the floor counselors, ultimately resulting in them being late for class.

Another one of our favorites was to squirt lighter fluid under their doors late at night when we knew they were asleep, light it with a match and yell, "fire!" and watch in delight as they ran out the door screaming.

But it wasn't just the class geeks who we picked on. The floor counselors, two nerdy seniors who lived on our floor and were paid to watch over us, were often the victims of our pranks, such as filling a large garbage call full of water, leaning it against their door and going back to our room and calling them anonymously on the phone, saying there was a fight going on down the hall or something to get them to come out of their room. Then we would watch as the counselors opened their door only to have gallons of water pour into their room. They hated us, and made no bones about it. They would often call us out of our rooms after one of the pranks, line us up against the wall and threaten to have us all expelled unless one of us confessed. Of course no one ever did, and all they could do was swear at us and tell us we'd better never do it again. What the heck, we figured, it was all in good fun, (for us anyway), and besides, they were getting paid for it.

Then there was Chopper, a small alligator that one of my dorm buddies, John Kelly, purchased downtown one day and kept in a tank in his room. One night, after arriving back from the bars, I decided to show off in front of the guys and picked Chopper up by the back of the neck.

"I saw once on a show about animals where if you rub an alligator's stomach it falls asleep," I said. (Actually I think I saw it on a Popeye cartoon). No one believed me so we made a bet. I started rubbing his stomach as I held him by the neck, and sure enough, his eyes began to close.

"See, I told you," I said proudly. "Pay up."

"I don't think he's really asleep," said one of the guys.

"Sure he is," I said. "Watch, I'll prove it."

I proceeded to stick my finger in his mouth. That turned out to be a mistake. Chopper clamped down on my finger and would not let go. I started yelling and finally flicked him off my finger, sending him flying across the room and hitting the wall. He lay motionless for a few minutes as we all stood over him.

"You killed Chopper," said John.

"He wouldn't let go of my finger. I had to do something," I replied, with blood squirting out of nine or ten teeth mark holes.

"Maybe he's not dead," said one of the guys in the room. But after picking him up and holding his limp body in his hands, John realized he was indeed dead. Heartbroken, he said a few parting words before flushing Chopper down the toilet.

"Maybe you should go to the hospital and get that finger looked at," said one of the guys.

"Let's go get Grover," someone said. "I think he's in pre-med. He'll know what to do."

Grover lived on another floor in our dorm and none of us knew him too well, not even whether "Grover" was his first name or last name. We just knew him as Grover.

Apparently he had been out partying that night too, and after taking a quick look at my finger he said in a somewhat slurred speech, "Just clean it, wrap it in bandages, take two aspirin and call me in the morning."

"Shouldn't he get a shot? He was bitten by an animal. Couldn't he get rabies or something?" said one of the guys.

"No way," replied Grover, swaying back and forth a bit. "Alligators don't get rabies." How he knew that we weren't quite sure, but we all nodded in agreement. "Besides, they're just tiny holes," he said. "It's not like half his hand got bitten off. He'll be fine." And then he left the room.

I took Grover's advice and washed the blood off my finger and bandaged it up. It healed in a few days, and I never developed rabies. But it did take several apologies and a few free beers on my part before John was speaking to me again.

I made plenty of friends over the course of that year, and met my share of girls. Even though Loras was an all-boys school there was an all-girls school about a mile away called Clarke that the guys visited often. It was also the place where I was to get arrested and actually spend time behind bars for the first and only time in my life.

A bunch of upper classmen had planned a panty raid, and told us freshmen it was a school tradition that they did every year. Of course my dorm buddies and I wanted to be included, and so we all "secretly" marched over to Clarke one night. There must have been several hundred of us all together.

We barely made it into the dorm lobbies and were heading toward the girls' rooms before hearing a sound we didn't expect or want to hear,—sirens.

Naturally we all made a break for it, scrambling out of the dorms and running for our lives. Most managed to escape. I was one of the unlucky ones.

"You're under arrest, son. Please step into the car," said the police officer.

"What did I do wrong, sir?" I asked him.

"Well, let's see. How about illegal trespassing, breaking and entering, and attempted theft for starters," he said. "And that's just off the top of my head. I'm sure I can come up with more."

The three of us in the back seat of the police car tried pleading our case. "It was a harmless college prank, officer. A yearly tradition."

"Try selling that to the captain downtown," he said sarcastically. And soon I was sitting along side 30 or so of my fellow classmates being booked by the policeman behind the desk at the station.

Then we were told to go into a jail cell, and the door closed on us with a loud clank. I was stunned, embarrassed, ashamed, and scared, all at the same time. What would my parents think of me if they found out? A simple prank that sounded like fun had suddenly turned into a nightmare. After an hour or so we were bailed out by none other than the dean of students at Loras, Father Kutsch, a grim, almost evil looking man, who, had he not chosen to join the priesthood, would have made it in Hollywood as a villain in horror movies.

"You boys are free to go, but I have your names and want to see each of you in my office first thing tomorrow morning," he said in an icy voice.

The visit with Father Kutsch wasn't much better than being in jail. He lectured us for nearly an hour on the evils of what we had done and that if we were ever caught in trouble again for any reason we would be expelled.

Fortunately, my parents were never called. But I was now on the dean's list, and not the good kind. I needed to lay low for a while and make sure to stay out of trouble. We heard the "masterminds" who planned the first panty raid were working on another attempt. I decided it best to skip that one.

We found out afterward that the "secret" panty raid had been leaked by a guy who had called his girlfriend at Clarke, and warned her that we were on our way, and to lock the door to her room. Apparently she decided to call the police too. We heard the guy was severely beaten.

Playing sports was a good way to stay out of trouble and so I joined both a flag football and a basketball intramural team, doing well in both. In fact, I was the leading scorer in the entire league my freshman year in basketball. I also got a part time job during the second semester, working for the school, mowing lawns and washing dishes to earn some extra cash.

However, despite my efforts to get through the year without having to deal with the dreaded dean again, I would have to face him one more time.

It was May, and I met a girl who I wanted to take to the spring prom. I took the bus home the weekend before and begged my parents to let me take one of their cars back to Dubuque so that I could have a car for the prom. At first they said no, saying it would leave them with only one car for the week. But after giving it some more consideration, they relented and figured they could get by. They even let me take the good car since they felt the other smaller one was just for driving in town and might not be safe on the highway.

Once again before handing the keys over to me, my parents laid out a strict set of rules. I was to park the car somewhere for the week and not use it until the prom. I agreed, thanked them, and was handed the keys.

However, once I got back to Loras the temptation was too irresistible to actually have a car and not make the most of it. I picked up four of my dorm buddies and we started driving around town. Unfortunately, while heading up a narrow hilly street with cars parked along both sides, I managed to run head-on into a car coming up from the other direction at the crest of the hill. None of us had our seat belts on, (it wasn't a law in those days), and out of instinct I put my knees up against the steering wheel to help brace myself for the impact, suffering only a few minor cuts. But my friend Denny, who was sitting in the front passenger seat, wasn't so lucky. He went through the windshield head-first and suffered some major injuries. The guys in the back seat were shaken up but not injured.

After tending to Denny, I walked around to the front of the car to check the extent of the damage. The front end was totally demolished. The police arrived soon, and after talking to the other driver and me wrote both of us out traffic tickets for negligent driving. At least I hadn't been drinking, otherwise I probably would have gotten a DUI on top of it. The police took Denny to the hospital and the rest of us back to our dorm. But the most difficult part was yet to come,— having to phone my parents.

I told them what happened and that I was OK but they said they would be there in an hour. It was the longest hour of my life. I waited in the front lobby for them to arrive. When they did they were naturally upset, but wanted to make sure I was OK before laying into me.

"We trusted you to park the car for the week, and within an hour you're out driving around with your friends," said my dad, rightfully angered. "Where is the car?"

"They towed it away. It's totaled," I reluctantly had to tell him. "I'm sorry," was all I could think to say.

"Well, at least you weren't hurt bad. It could have been worse," said my mom." Then I had to tell them about my friend who had to be taken to the hospital. Later my parents would receive a letter from his parents' lawyer who was suing us. The case was eventually settled out of court. I don't how much my parents had to pay, but my guess is it was a pretty healthy sum. Fortunately, after a few days in the hospital Denny turned out OK.

And last but not least was the phone call I received the

next day from none other than Father Kutsch, who wanted to see me in his office right away.

"I heard that you were driving a car on campus and got into an accident," he said in that creepy voice of his. "I don't see in our records that you registered your car to park on campus, which is in violation of the rules. You will need to pay a fine and purchase a parking permit to put on your car."

"No need for that." I replied. "The car is sitting in the junk yard."

Fortunately, I don't think he remembered me from the panty raid incident. At least he didn't mention it or have me expelled.

My parents eventually started speaking to me again, and no doubt were glad that the semester was nearly over, and I would be coming home before getting into any more trouble.

My grades had improved slightly that semester, but not good enough to qualify for my sophomore year unless I took summer school classes.

"I don't want to go to summer school," I said to Eddie. "I need to get a job and start paying my parents back for all I owe them, like having to buy a new car, paying the lawsuit settlement, and all my fines. I can't ask them for more money to go to summer school."

"If you quit school you'll get drafted, man," said Eddie. It was 1968 and the war in Vietnam was not only dragging on, it was escalating. The only thing keeping me from being draft eligible was that I was a college student.

"What the hell am I going to do?" I said.

"Well, you could always volunteer for the military," he

replied. "At least that way you would have your choice of what branch of service you wanted to get into, and maybe even where you wanted to be stationed. It beats getting drafted into the Army and getting your ass shot at on the front lines in Nam."

Eddie was onto something. After thinking about it overnight, I decided to go downtown and visit the local Naval recruiting office. My dad was a Navy man and I figured being on a ship was better than being in some jungle.

"I would like to join the Navy," I said to the recruiter. And soon I was taking tests and filling out forms.

"What line of work would you be interested in?" he asked.

"I want to be a gunner," I quickly replied.

"A gunner?" he said, surprised. "Why would you want to be that?"

"Who wouldn't want to be a gunner?" I thought to myself, and said to him, "So I can shoot down enemy planes and ships."

He just looked at me and shook his head. "You haven't given this a lot of thought, have you? The Navy has many fields you could get into that would provide you with a good education that you could make use of as a career once you got out of the service. Here's a pamphlet. I would suggest looking through it and deciding on a career choice."

While making up my mind as to what career to choose, the semester ended, and my parents came to take me home.

On the way back my mom said, "So, what have you been up to lately?"

"I decided to quit school and join the Navy," I replied, waiting for a response, hopefully a positive one. But instead there was only stunned silence.

Chapter 7

~

It didn't take long for me to realize my parents were less than thrilled with my plan. After telling them that I had been to the Naval recruiting office and had taken tests and signed some papers, my dad pulled over at the next exit and turned the car around.

"Where are we going?" I asked.

"To the Naval recruiting office," he shot back.

Once again I had brought my mom to the brink of tears and incurred the wrath of my dad.

"I thought you would be happy," I said. "I was just trying to save you money."

"What are you talking about?" they replied.

"Because of my grades I can't go back next year unless I take summer school classes," I said. "I figured if I went into the Navy you wouldn't have to worry about paying any more money for my education. I would be getting paid and could send you money for all the things I've cost you this year."

While they had to admit it was a nice gesture on my part to think of them, they wanted me to finish my education and get a degree, no matter what the cost.

When we arrived at the recruiting office my dad and I went in while my mom stayed in the car. After introducing himself to the recruiter, his first question was, "Did my son sign anything binding or can he still change his mind?"

"No," said the recruiter. He hasn't signed anything official yet. He can still change his mind if he wants to."

That was the answer my dad was hoping to hear. "My son and I will discuss this and get back to you," he said to the recruiter, and once again we were headed for home, discussing the pros and cons of me joining the Navy the entire trip.

"You were in the Navy," I said to my dad. "I thought you would be proud of me to follow in your footsteps."

"That's not the point," he answered. "Your mother and I want for you to have choices in life, and the best way to give yourself that chance is to get a college degree. Don't worry about paying us back or about how much it will cost to go to summer school. Let us worry about that part."

"Please listen to your father," said my mom. "We don't want you going into the Navy and having to be sent who knows where. You could get caught up in the middle of the war and be sent someplace dangerous."

We continued to discuss it for several weeks before I finally gave in. "OK, I'll sign up for summer school," I told my parents, with mixed emotions. As much as I enjoyed my freshman year in college, the idea of seeing the world, (not to mention shooting down enemy planes and ships), had it's appeal. But I called the Naval recruiter and told him I changed my mind and that he had to find another gunner.

I signed up for two classes at St. Ambrose, the local college, and if I passed them I would qualify for my sophomore year at Loras. I felt like I was back in high school, living at home and constantly being told to do my homework. But I managed to pass the classes and also get on at Alcoa again to earn some money, which I gave most of to my parents.

In between going to school and working, I managed to find time to hang out with my old high school buddies, and played poker and drank beer, just like the good old days.

That summer flew by, and before I knew it I was headed back up to Loras. Eddie was surprised to see me, thinking I was headed for the Navy. We ended up being roommates again.

It didn't take long for me to remember how great college life was, and that my parents were right in talking me out of joining the Navy. Plus, because I managed to stay in school, I avoided being draft eligible, at least for the time being.

The late '60s had become turbulent times, with the assassinations of Martin Luther King and Bobby Kennedy, the violence during the Democratic National Convention in Chicago, and the election of Richard Nixon, who campaigned against the war but then escalated it even further after taking office. "Tricky Dick" was one of the most hated political figures of our time, especially among the young people who feared they would be forced into a war they could not understand nor wanted any part of. It was the most unpopular war in our history, not only among the younger generation, but among many politicians and spokesmen who voiced their opinion against the war.

Student protests exploded everywhere around the country, and riots often ensued. It was the "Hardhats" versus the "Hippies," and although it was difficult for those of us in school to fully comprehend it at the time, we were living through one of the most violent eras in American history.

Nixon continued to expand the war and called for more troops in 1969. None of us felt safe anymore, whether we were in college or not. That December he initiated the infamous "birthday draft," which determined who would be drafted according to the day they were born. They put 365 cards in a bin, containing each date of the year, and pulled them out one by one. Analysts calculated that if your card was chosen in the bottom half you were probably safe. If not, you were likely to be drafted.

I vividly remember sitting in front of the TV with my friends that night, all of us crossing our fingers and praying that our card would not be drawn early. It didn't take long for the suspense to end for me. I was number 46.

"46?" I said, slamming my fist against a chair. "365 frigging days out of the year and they pick me 46th." Even though I had been willing to join the Navy a mere few months before, the thought of fighting in some jungle in Vietnam not only scared the hell out of me, but had become a war that, like most people of my generation, I was totally opposed to. My only hope was that my college status would continue to keep me out of the draft.

My driver's license expired that fall so I took the bus home one weekend to get it renewed. I went to the license bureau figuring to take the eye exam, get my picture taken, pay the cost of the new license, and be out of there. But after handing my license to the woman behind the desk, she took one look at it and said, "Please have a seat over there, sir."

"Why?" I asked, after already having waited my turn in line for an hour.

"Please sir, just take a seat. Someone will be with you shortly."

I still didn't get it, that was until a police officer came over to where I was sitting and said, "I see you have tampered with your license. Are you aware that is against the law?"

And that's when it hit me,—Eddie Quinn. I had totally forgotten about that night at school when he changed the date on my license.

"I'm sorry, sir," I said, trying to think of something, anything to get me out of this mess. "Someone tried to change the date on my license a few years ago and I totally forgot about it."

"Why would someone want to do that?" he replied, knowing full well why.

"I don't know, sir," was the only answer I could think of off the top of my head.

"Did this person take your license and change it without your knowledge or consent?"

"No, sir," I had to admit. He had me in a corner and there was no way out.

"Then I am going to have to revoke your license for six

months, at which time you may apply for a new one." He took my old license and walked away.

One more headache for my mom and dad. I had to call them and tell them what happened, and that they had to come pick up me since I couldn't drive home. The only good news was that I didn't have to pay a fine or go to jail, and I wasn't going to need the use of a car much anyway, since I was going back to Loras for the second semester.

Aside from the daily threat of receiving a letter from Uncle Sam, I vowed to make the remainder of my sophomore year better than ever, attending classes more, while still managing to have a good time, and most importantly, to stay out of trouble and avoid Father Kutsch at all cost. I continued to hang out with most of my same buddies from my freshman year. But I was to meet some new people too, like Pat Sullivan, and Tom DeMateo, who would turn out to be among my closest friends. And there was a girl I met who I would end up spending the rest of my life with.

I was hanging around the school library one afternoon, looking through old copies of Sports Illustrateds, when I spotted a cute looking girl I didn't recall ever seeing before. I decided to go up to her and introduce myself. "Hi, my name's Pat. Do you go to school around here?"

"Hi, I'm Mimi," she replied with a smile that I was to become fond of. "I'm a freshman at Clarke. My real name is Mary but everyone knows me by the nickname my brother gave me when we were kids."

"So what brings you to the Loras library?" I asked.

"I'm looking for a book that I couldn't find at the Clarke library," she responded.

"Well, if it's a Sports Illustrated, I know exactly where to find it," I said, trying my best to say something clever.

That made her laugh, which was a good sign. We seemed to be hitting it off pretty well so I went for it. "Loras has a home game tonight. If you're not doing anything, would you like to go with me?"

"Sure," she said. And, as the saying goes, the rest is history. We went to the basketball game that night and then out for a bite to eat afterward.

I would be making quite a few trips to Clarke over the next several months, and even discovered a shortcut through the woods that cut the trip in half. (Actually I wasn't the first to discover it. There was a well-worn path that had been used many times over the years by many guys).

When I wasn't visiting Mimi or going to classes or hanging out downtown in a local establishment with my friends, I was playing intramural sports. I played flag football again, and was asked by some guys I didn't know all that well who lived in our dorm if I wanted to join their basketball team.

They called their team the "Chaparrals," and were good their freshman year, but were looking for a big man in the middle. I was their guy. We were a balanced team, with plenty of shooters and ball handlers. We went through the regular season winning our division, and making the tournament.

We won our first few tournament games handily, although I suffered what turned out to be pulled ligaments in my shoulder during one of the games, and was told by a doctor to keep it in a sling for a couple weeks.

"A couple weeks?" said one of my teammates. "We've got some tough games coming up. Are you sure you can't play?"

"I wish I could, but I can't even raise my arm," I replied, extremely disappointed.

"That's OK," said one of the guys. "We've got two games this week and if we can win those we'll be in the championship. Maybe you'll be ready by then."

We did end up winning those two games with me sitting on the sidelines. The big game was coming up in a few days, against the top-seeded senior team, no less. My shoulder was still hurting, but I was bound and determined I was going to play.

I decided to go see the Loras team trainer at the school gym to see if he could help me. He was a kind old guy nicknamed "Doc," and after explaining my injury and telling him we were playing for the championship, he said, "Well, let's see what I can do for you." He taped up my shoulder, tight enough to relieve most of the pain, but also flexible enough to allow me to move my arm.

"How does that feel?" he said.

"It feels good," I replied. Fortunately, I was right handed, and the injury was to my left shoulder, so shooting the ball didn't bother me. It was when I had to lift my left arm to rebound where I felt the pain. But it definitely felt better than before.

"I think that might just work," I said. "Thanks a lot, Doc. I really appreciate it."

"Good luck tomorrow," he said with a smile. "Maybe I'll come to the game and watch you."

When I told my teammates what Doc had done for me and that I was ready to play, one of the guys said, "We're going to win it. We're going to win the championship. We may be the underdogs against the hot shot seniors, but if they think they're going kick some sophomore ass, they're in for a big surprise." That pumped us up. We were ready to go.

The big game finally arrived, and the people in charge of the league chose to play it in the big gym where the Loras team played, rather than in the smaller intramural gym where we had played our games up to that point. They even broadcast the game over the local school radio station. The place was packed. Standing room only. The senior team we were about to play had been together for four years but had never won the championship, having finished runner up the previous year, and highly motivated to go out winners.

The game went back and forth, with neither team leading by more than a few points the entire game. I was holding my own, scoring, rebounding, and blocking shots. The adrenaline was pumping and I was feeling no pain. The game went down to the wire, with us pulling it out at the end for a 67-65 win and the championship.

It was only after the game that I felt the pain in my shoulder. But it wasn't anything that 10 or 12 beers at our favorite bar couldn't cure. We celebrated well into the night, and while it might not have been for the NCAA championship, it felt like it to us. Although I've lost touch with most of them over the years, those of us who participated in that night's victory and celebration will be forever linked, and the names of Mike Quinn, Kevin Tritz, Gordy Pizarik, Ron Reid, Jerry Rolling, and Bob Shoger will remain a lasting part of one of the most memorable moments of my life.

I would spend the remainder of that year dividing my time between Loras and Clarke, making that shortcut through the woods to see Mimi many times. We didn't have transportation or much spending money, and Mimi didn't care much for going downtown to the bars anyway, so our dates usually consisted of buying milk and cookies, and watching TV in the Clarke dorm. I was falling in love for the first time in my life, and gradually spent less time with my buddies, and more time with Mimi.

But that spring I was to fall in love with someone else too,—The Chicago Cubs. I had followed the "Loveable Losers" every year since my dad got me interested in them, but the 1969 season was different. They started out hot and were in first place through April and May. With guys like Billy Williams, Glenn Beckert, Don Kessinger, Ron Santo, and of course the legendary Ernie Banks, they were soon becoming the powerhouse of the National League.

My sophomore year came to an end, much more successfully than did my freshman year. My grades had improved, and I managed to stay out of trouble, and never had to visit the dean's office. Overall, my cumulative grade point average was marginal at best because of the slow start I got off to, and I could not decide what to major in, or what courses to take when I came back in the fall. But at that point, I wasn't going to worry about it. I was going to have a great summer.

Like the line in Bryan Adam's song *Summer of '69,'* "Those were the best days of my life," the summer of 1969 was one I will always remember. Although I worked at Alcoa again that summer, I managed to find plenty of time to spend with my friends, and especially with Mimi. She lived in Park Forest, a suburb on the south side of Chicago, and I would spend many days visiting both her and Wrigley Field. I saw many games that summer, mostly with Mimi, and some with friends or with my dad. It was a crazed atmosphere at Wrigley, like nothing I had ever seen before. The Cubs remained in first place for nearly the entire summer, with Santo clicking his heels after each win.

In mid August they held what seemed like an insurmountable nine game lead. But then things started to crumble. The New York Mets, who nobody took seriously up until that point, suddenly couldn't lose, and were gaining ground almost every day on the suddenly floundering Cubs. Fans began chanting prayers, like "Hail Mary, full of grace, keep the Mets in second place." But all the prayers and rosary beads in Chicago couldn't stop the inevitable. By September the Mets had taken over first place, and the Cubs would not catch them. It took me a long time to get over the way that season ended, but it still couldn't spoil one of the best summers of my life.

As for school, I had to make a decision. Facing marginal grades, not enough credit hours, no plans on what courses to take or what to major in, I couldn't decide which direction to go. It was a friend of mine from high school, Gary Calkins, who offered me the advice that would ultimately make my decision.

He had gone to a local community college and earned a two year degree in applied science, and found a good paying job as a computer programmer. "Computers," he said.

"That's where the future is." You go to school for two years and earn a degree. They even help place you in a job afterward. The demand for programmers is sky high right now, and it pays good money. You can't go wrong."

As much as I would miss Loras and my friends, and especially Mimi, Gary's advice made sense. I would earn a degree like my parents wanted, and save them a ton of money by living at home. I discussed it with them, and they agreed that it seemed like a good choice. I applied at Scott Community College that August.

And so my college days at Loras had come to an end. They were two of the best years of my life, and would leave lasting memories which I still think about to this day.

Chapter 8

~

My days at Scott Community College were quite a change from the crazed atmosphere at Loras. It felt like high school all over again, being told to do my homework, waking up to the alarm clock, (and not being allowed to shut it off and go back to sleep), attending classes from 8:00 A.M. to 4:00 P.M. every day, and once again eating my mom's overcooked meals. But at least my parents let me have a car most weekends in order to reunite with my friends and Mimi in Dubuque.

In fact, Scott was nothing like Loras in many ways. It was a business school, and the people who attended it were all business. Other than joining them for lunch on occasion, I rarely hung out with anyone socially there.

By fall of 1969 most of my old high school buddies were away at school, so I didn't see them much anymore. The old poker playing days were pretty much gone, and replaced with playing bridge with my family. My dad also taught me the game of chess, which I really took to, and referred to it as "the perfect game." Besides it's similar but simpler version, checkers, chess was the only game I knew of where there was no luck involved. There were no cards to draw or dice to roll. It was simply a game matching wits, with no one having an advantage over the other. The winner won because of pure skill, which was what I liked about it. My dad was my only completion for a while. No one else in the family played, nor did any of my friends, with the exception of Mike McCarthy. Whenever he was home from school we would get together to play chess, and became very competitive opponents over the years.

That November I turned 21, and if I were up at Loras, it would have meant a night of serious partying with my friends. We had a small family party, but just when I was feeling sorry for myself not being able to celebrate my big day with my buddies, my dad surprised me by suggesting we go out on the town and hit the bars. He and I toasted many times that night to my 21st birthday, and we ended up having a great time together. It was the first time I remember thinking of my dad as my friend as well as my father.

Mimi and I had fallen seriously in love, and began talking about spending the rest of our lives together. We would talk for hours on the phone or send each other mushy love letters when we weren't together. But then one day I received a letter I didn't want to see. It was the letter I had feared.

It was from the U.S. Government instructing me to report to Des Moines for a physical and subsequent draft into the military. I tried appealing, writing to them indicating I was attending a technical college and should be considered exempt. But my appeal was denied. Soon I was on a bus with a bunch of other guys my age headed to Des Moines. This was it, I thought. I was on my way to Vietnam.

We all spent the night in a barracks, and the next morning got in line and proceeded to have several doctors examine us. It was while taking my blood pressure that my fate suddenly took a dramatic turn.

"That is extremely high for a person your age, said the doctor. "Are you aware that you have high blood pressure?"

"No," I said. "I had no idea. Is it that bad?"

"Bad enough to keep you out of the military," he responded. "I suggest you see a doctor and get on some medication as soon as possible."

Did I hear him right? Did he actually say what I thought he said? I was being rejected for military duty? I didn't know whether to be worried about having high blood pressure or be elated because I flunked the physical. I do remember having a smile on my face the entire trip back from Des Moines.

After getting back and telling my parents and Mimi the news, I scheduled an appointment with our family doctor. After taking my blood pressure he said it was slightly high for someone my age, but not enough to be on medication. Apparently the fear of being drafted had elevated my blood pressure past the allowable limit for military induction. I felt like the luckiest person on the face of the earth. I wasn't going to "get my ass shot at in Vietnam," as Eddie had put it. I was free. Free to follow through with my plans to continue school, earn my degree, and eventually get married.

My parents had met Mimi several times when I brought her home with me for a weekend, or when she took the train in from Chicago during the summer. They really seemed to like her, and when I told them how I felt about her and wanted to marry her someday, they were happy.

That Christmas I drove to Park Forest to spend a few days with Mimi, and brought something along with me,—an engagement ring. I asked her to marry me and her answer was yes. When we told her mom and dad the news, they seemed to be as happy as mine about our decision.

We made tentative plans to get married in the summer. Looking back on it now, it probably would have been more practical for us to wait until I graduated and found a job. But we were young and in love, and didn't want to wait another year to be together. I had fallen in love with that sparkle in her eyes when she smiled, and her always cheery attitude. She was down to earth, totally without pretense, and enjoyed life, even the simplest things, like going for long walks, or gazing up at the stars at night and pointing out the constellations. I had never felt like this before in my life.

We talked about the idea of her not returning to Clarke for her second semester and getting a job instead. After discussing it with her parents, they agreed, and she wound up working at a local Jewel Food Store in Park Forest.

And so our days in Dubuque had officially come to an end. I would still drive up there once in a while just to keep in touch with my buddies, but for the most part I spent whatever free time I had going to see Mimi or her coming to see me. I was getting through school and headed toward my degree, while she was saving the money she earned at work for our future.

By the spring of 1970 we were making wedding plans. I was about to start a new life, and with it came new responsibilities and doing things I never had to do before,— like sending out wedding invitations, making a list of who to invite to the wedding, who to ask to be in the wedding party, going apartment hunting, furniture shopping, finding a car, and figuring out where to go on our honeymoon.

Thanks to my grandfather, the honeymoon part was taken care of for us. He owned a cottage in St. Petersburg, Florida and his wedding gift to us was to let us have it for a week. He even let us have the use of his car that he kept down there.

I ended up buying a car of my own that summer, a white 1964 Chevy that I was quite proud of. Having a driver's license was one thing, but it was nothing compared to owning your own car.

Mimi and I picked out an affordable apartment in Bettendorf, and bought the necessary items to fill it. It already came with a refrigerator, oven, and washer and dryer. The rest was up to us, and we spent the money Mimi had saved up on a couch, chair, TV, kitchen table and chairs. My parents gave us a bed and dresser set as a wedding gift.

The big day finally arrived on August 15th. My best man was Mike McCarthy, my Colorado traveling buddy and favorite chess opponent. The wedding came off without a hitch, and on that Saturday afternoon, Mimi AuBuchon had officially become Mimi Triplett. We spent the night in downtown Chicago and left for Florida the next morning.

Our week in St. Petersburg was wonderful. My grandfather's cottage was one block from the ocean. We would wake up in the morning, grab a bite to eat, and head for the beach. The weather was perfect, and we enjoyed every minute of it. The week went by fast and we hated the thought of leaving, but at the same time we were excited about the idea of living in our apartment together and starting our new lives as husband and wife.

Mimi was able to transfer to a Jewel store in town. It was difficult at times only having one car, with her working and me going to school, but we made it work, just like we made everything work back in those days.

She was making good money at Jewel, and I got a part time job working as a janitor after school. It seemed like money was never much of a factor for us, even though I was still going to school and didn't have a full time job. My parents paid for my tuition, and we had paid cash for our car and furniture, so our only payments were basically for the apartment, utilities and food.

I graduated in the spring of 1971, participating in the cap and gown ceremony and receiving my diploma. While it been a struggle at times over the years, I had finally earned the college degree that my parents had wanted.

I immediately began looking for a job, but it wasn't as easy as Gary had promised me. The school gave me some references but I was having trouble finding anything for the first few months. Meanwhile, I continued to work at Scott full time at night as a maintenance man/janitor.

When I wasn't job hunting, I spent much of that summer playing golf. One beautiful summer day I asked Mimi to go with me since she had the day off. She had never so much as held a golf club in her hand before and didn't want to go, fearing she would end up embarrassing both of us.

"It's a weekday. It won't be crowded," I said. "Besides, it's a public course and anyone can play, even those who are just learning the game. Come with me. It will be fun."

"But I don't have any golf clubs," she said.

"We can rent some," I replied. "Don't worry about not playing well or being embarrassed. We'll just do it for the fun of it."

I finally talked her into it. We rented some clubs for her and headed for the first tee. Unfortunately, the course was more crowded than I thought it would be, and the starter paired us up with two other guys. That didn't help Mimi's confidence. Nor did the fact that the they had rented a cart while Mimi and I were walking, which would slow them up. And they were obviously good players, both hitting their tee shots 250 yards down the middle of the fairway. I went next and hit a decent drive. Then it was Mimi's turn.

As she put her ball on the tee and prepared to swing, I remember thinking, "Please God, just let her make contact, even if it only goes 20 yards."

She swung and missed the ball by three feet.

"Oh God," said one of the guys in our group, both of them rolling their eyes in disgust.

"That's OK," I said to Mimi. "Try it again. Just relax and keep your eye on the ball."

She swung and missed again. Then came a voice over the loudspeaker. "Triplett, get in here." The starter was actually calling me into the clubhouse. "Why didn't you tell me she couldn't play?" he said, perturbed.

"This is a public course," I replied, equally perturbed.

"She's learning the game. She has as much right to play as anyone."

"All right, but tell her to hurry it up. We're getting backed up because of her," he said.

I went back out to the tee and tried to encourage Mimi to try it again while explaining to the two guys that this was her first time out and she was learning how to play. They weren't too receptive to the idea of having to play with a woman who couldn't hit the ball, and said they would go ahead of us after the first hole, which made me even madder and Mimi more embarrassed.

"That's OK," she said. "I'll just walk with you."

Now I had two goals. One was trying to convince Mimi to at least hit a few shots when we got closer to the greens, and the other was to beat those two bastards. I managed to hold my own with them, and although they kept their own scores, I'm pretty sure I outscored them. At least I shut them up. Meanwhile, Mimi was content to walk with me and not hit another shot the rest of the round. In fact, it would be the last time she would ever swing a golf club.

The year ended with me still not finding a computer job, and continuing to work nights at Scott. I even tried interviewing in Chicago and St. Louis, where my friend Steve lived, but with no success. Mimi continued to work at Jewel and we were still doing OK financially. We ended the year with a New Year's Eve bash at our apartment with our best friends, Gary Calkins, who kept swearing I would got a job soon, and his wife Nancy, and John Regan, who I knew from high school but didn't hang around with much until we went to Loras together, and like me, married a Clarke girl named Connie.

1972 would bring about many changes. I finally found a job that spring, working as a computer operator for an insurance company named Bituminous. Mimi was pregnant with our first child, due to be born in August. Since we lived in a one bedroom apartment, we decided to start looking for another place to live. We ended up renting a house in Davenport, and despite having a hole in the roof that we didn't notice until after we moved in, it did the job.

After partying at the Calkins' house one night until 1:00 A.M, Mimi woke me up a few hours later to tell me her water had broken. I wasn't sure exactly what that meant, but I figured we were on our way to the hospital. I pulled into a parking spot in the visitor's lot some 100 feet from the front door before Mimi told me that this qualified as a case where I could drive up to the emergency room door.

It was still old school as far as the delivery process in those days, with Mimi in the delivery room and me pacing back and forth in the waiting room. At approximately 6:00 A.M, on August 13th, 1972, Matthew Patrick was born. Now I was not only a husband, but a father as well.

Chapter 9

~

We lived in the house with the hole in the roof until the fall of 1972, when we purchased our first real house. It was a modest little three bedroom ranch, but to us it was home, and would be for the next seven years.

It was strange at first having a third person in the house, but it didn't take long to get used to Matt. Light haired with blue eyes like his mother, he was a joy to have around. We would just sit and watch him for hours at a time. We didn't even need a TV. He was our entertainment.

And I quickly got used to holding him the proper way, feeding him, and even changing his diapers on occasion. I was learning how to become a father.

I continued to work as a computer operator rather than a programmer, which is what I had earned my degree in. The program manager there promised me a job as soon as one opened up. I had started out working a normal eight hour shift but then went to the night shift, working 13 hours at a time, three nights a week, from 4 P.M. to 5 A.M. The nights were long, but having four days off made up for it. And I was pretty much my own boss, being the only one in the building for most of my shift. That lasted for three years until I was eventually able to transfer into the programming department.

In 1975 Mimi was pregnant with our second child, due the following January. Things had advanced in the birthing process since Matt was born. The father was now allowed to be in the delivery room during the birth, and we attended weekly meetings called "Lamaze," where a teacher taught both the mother and father how to cope with the process of giving birth.

She taught things such as how to breath properly during contractions, and for the father to act as coach during the technique, timing the length of the contractions, and helping teach the correct breathing process. She also suggested ways of passing time while in the labor room, such as playing board games like scrabble.

Mimi was overdue, so the doctor decided to induce labor. By the time I dropped her off, (this time at the emergency door), parked the car, and made it into the labor room, Mimi was fully dilated and ready to go.

As I entered the room her first words to me were, "No scrabble." The nurse dressed me in a cap, gown and mask and wheeled Mimi into the delivery room. Within minutes, Michael John Triplett was born, with me watching in awe.

Mike was born with dark black hair and dark brown eyes,

just the opposite of Matt. In fact, they were total opposites in many ways. Matt was quiet and passive for the most part, while Mike was louder and more ornery. Matt was normally content to play on his own, coloring and drawing pictures. Mike was, well, a handful, full of vigor and given to occasional tantrums.

As they grew older they had their moments, often fighting with each other. Matt was the older brother who felt superior to his younger counterpart, while Mike was not willing to give an inch when he felt he was right. I remember having to separate them and settle their disputes on many occasions.

Matt was more shy and hesitant when it came to going to school, while Mike was more headstrong and often infuriated his teachers. He wasn't a troublemaker, he was just being himself, and when he felt like he was right, whether at home or at school, he let his feelings be known. I clearly remember the day he came home from school and dropped to the floor, saying "That's as good as I can be."

Matt became an expert at drawing maps and making calendars in his early days. He was fascinated by the street names he looked up in the phone book, and wanted us to drive him around town to find the streets so that he could mark them on his map.

Mike was much more adventurous and daring. We were watching a show on TV one night called *That's Incredible*. In a particular episode they tied a man up tightly to a chair with ropes and somehow he was able to free himself within minutes. Fascinated by this, Mike wanted us to tie him to a chair with ropes just like the guy on TV. We went along with it, of course tying the ropes loosely so that he could easily escape and be content.

But after freeing himself in a few minutes, he was not

only proud of his accomplishment, he wanted to go on the show.

"You can't go on the show," we said. "You're four years old. The show is in New York, and we have to go to work. We can't take you."

"That's OK," said Mike. I'll go by myself."

"How will you know how to get there?" we said, trying our best to talk him out of his crazy notion.

"I'll figure it out," he said confidently. It took us a good two hours to finally convince him he couldn't go.

We always figured Mike would turn out to be a lawyer. Whenever he felt we were wrong and he was right, he would argue his case for hours without giving in. Meanwhile, the sibling rivalry continued between he and Matt, with Mimi and I having to be judge and jury to break up their seemingly endless disputes.

But Mike did provide us with some humorous moments too, one of which was at a science fair at Matt's grade school. As we were wandering around looking at all the exhibits the students provided, we stopped by a girl who had a brain in a jar. Of course Mimi and I realized that it was an animal's brain, but Mike, being typically curious, decided to ask the girl where she got the brain.

"From my dad," she said.

To which Mike replied in a voice loud enough for most of the people in the room to hear, "I didn't know your dad died."

Mike continued to both entertain and frustrate us for the next several years. I recall taking him to a movie he really wanted to see called *Spaceballs*. I wasn't all that excited about seeing it but I did it as a favor to him. There was a scene during the movie where Dark Helmet, based on the *Star Wars'* Darth Vader character, played by Rick Moranis, told the captain to stop the spaceship, and ended up flying across the room and smashing into the wall. I burst into an uncontrolled laughter and could not stop. Mike tried to restrain me and told me if I didn't stop laughing the usher would kick us out of the theater. It became a memorable moment for both us that we still reminisce about to this day. I still have the movie on video, and laugh just as hard every time I see that scene.

Living in our own house did provide me with the opportunity to pursue something I began when I was a small kid, building things in our basement. But instead of buses and airplanes and automatic pin setters, it was walls and doors and paneling, and this time I had the knowledge and equipment to be able to do it.

When we first moved in, our basement was nothing more than one huge empty room with cement walls and floors and cheap light fixtures. Other than a washer, dryer and a furnace, the downstairs was one large barren room.

That was until I decided to liven it up a bit. First I built a wall and door to close off the washer, dryer and furnace and make it a separate room. Then Mimi and I put tile down on the floor to add some color and brighten up the place. And my greatest accomplishment was constructing a wall and a door in the back half of the basement and stocking the room with a pool table, refrigerator, TV and stereo. I called it my "game room."

We painted the walls a brick red and added curtains on the

windows, and would later add carpet and some furniture to the front half of the downstairs, where the kids would play and have friends over. We eventually had turned what was once a boring basement into three separate rooms. I was proud of myself.

But there was one more project that I had no business attempting. That involved electricity, which I knew nothing about other than how to screw in a light bulb. My goal was to replace the current light fixtures with some nicer ones. I climbed up on a ladder and pulled the chain on the light fixture, turning off the light bulb, and thinking that turned off the power to the light switch. I was wrong. The last thing I remember was taking a screw driver and attempting to remove the old fixture.

Mimi came running down the stairs and found me lying on my back against the wall.

"What happened?" she said. I heard you scream and then there was a loud crash. That was me falling off the ladder and hitting the wall after being shocked. It would be the last time I ever attempted anything that had to do with electricity.

In fact, I began to realize that, while I was pretty handy working with wood, and that I could do my own painting, when it came to anything mechanical, I was deficient, to say the least. Ironically, the boy who once attempted to build airplanes, escalators and automatic pin setters had grown up to be a person who couldn't fix a leaky faucet to save his life. My dad had passed down many wonderful things to me, but unfortunately, things like car repairs, plumbing, electrical work, and fixing appliances were not among them.

I soon gained a reputation among friends and co-workers of my inability to perform even the simplest of mechanical tasks. It became sort of a standing joke, which I didn't mind, and would even tell them stories such as the infamous light fixture incident.

I recall one day at work my friend Reed telling me that he needed to tune up his lawn mower, to which I replied, "Mine needs tuning up too, but it's so expensive and it takes forever to get it back when you take it someplace. Maybe I'll do it myself this year."

Trying to keep a straight face, he said, "You're going to tune up your own lawn mower, really?"

"Sure, why not," I replied. "Change the oil, get a new filter, spark plug, sharpen the blade. I can't be that tough. I'm going to give it a shot."

"Could you do me a favor?" Reed asked. "Could you videotape it for me?"

Despite starting out with good intentions that following weekend, I ended up having to take it into the shop, and Reed never got to see the videotape.

I now had a house, a job, a wife, two children, and all the responsibilities that went with it. The only problem was I still didn't feel like a grown up, ready to settle down yet. I would continue to get together with my old buddies to play poker or hang out in bars or party with the Calkins and Regans until the wee hours of the morning. I was basically still an irresponsible young man with plenty of responsibilities, which I left mostly to my wife.

I went with John to South Bend one Saturday to see my first Notre Dame game and celebrate with Irish fans well into the night, to the Final Four basketball tournament in St. Louis with Steve and John, and on a bus trip to a Bulls game in Chicago with several of my friends, complete with coolers full of beer that we started drinking as soon as we got on the bus that morning, and didn't stop until we got home late that night.

It never dawned on me during my '20s that I should have acted any differently. I thought the purpose of life was to have fun, and that's pretty much how I lived it. I played park board league basketball, softball, flag football, golf every weekend, and bowled several nights a week in a league. Looking back on it now I realize that while I was having fun, I left most of the chores and taking care of the boys up to my wife. And Mimi being Mimi, she seldom complained.

As for me, It wasn't a case where I neglected my family or was abusive toward them. I loved my wife and kids as much as anyone, especially Mimi, who held the family together, despite all she had to do. We would all go to movies, to a restaurant on occasion, and play board games together. I played ball with the boys in the yard, and even taught them to play chess, just like my dad taught me.

The problem was that I didn't help out around the house very much, or pick up the kids from school, or help take care of them when they were sick, or watch them when Mimi was tired out from having to go to work, and then having to do the cleaning, the laundry, the dishes, and, with the exception of "party toast," the cooking.

Party toast was my specialty, and I served it to the boys whenever Mimi was at work. It consisted of making several pieces of toast, putting either peanut butter, jelly, or cinnamon sugar on them, and cutting them into diagonal shapes, thus putting the "party" in party toast. That worked for several years until the boys grew old enough to realize that party toast was a scam that I led them to believe was something special when in reality it was nothing more than regular toast shaped differently. At that point I had to step it up a notch by going to hot dogs and TV dinners.

Eventually, I would learn to do more of the cooking in my later years, something I really enjoyed. Naturally I was in charge of the grill, a tradition that seems to belong to men only. In fact, I cannot recall ever seeing a woman cooking on the grill.

But I also began cooking other meals too, such as rigatoni, oven baked pasta, chicken nachos, home-made pizza, meatball sandwiches, and enchiladas.

Mimi was still the expert when it came to my favorite meal,—turkey dinner, with all the fixings. I would pile everything on my plate, mix it all together, and pour gravy over the whole thing. I thought that was the way you were supposed to do it until I watched my daughter-in-law, Andrea, one Thanksgiving, not only keeping all her food separate, but eating all of her vegetables first, then all of her potatoes, then all of her turkey. I couldn't believe it.

It's funny how people's eating habits differ. I've seen my friend, Reed, a thin, 150 pound guy, devour an entire large pizza in one sitting. I've seen one of the boy's friends, Ryan, do the same thing as Andrea, and eat everything on his plate separately. The difference with him was that he ate not only everything on his plate, but everything in sight. He was one of those guys who, when he was done with his meal, would ask other people at the table, "Are you going to finish that?"

I remember asking Ryan once if there was anything he didn't like, half kidding, and expecting him to say at least a few things that he didn't care for. But after thinking about it for a few minutes, he said, in all seriousness, "Horseradish."

"You will literally eat anything that is put in front of you except horseradish?" I asked.

"Yep," he replied. "There's just something about horseradish I don't like."

Then there was the opposite extreme. Mimi's mom, a notorious light eater, once served us tacos for dinner when I came to visit many years ago.

"Tacos?" I said. "Sounds great. I love tacos."

We were served one taco each, which I ate in 30 seconds. Waiting for my next taco, I realized there were none left. She had prepared one taco per person, thinking that was plenty to tide us over. Trying to be polite, I didn't say anything. However, I do recall Mimi and I going out as soon as her mom went to bed, and pigging out at a fast food restaurant.

Chapter 10

~

In 1978 things began to change. My dad suffered a heart attack that fall at the age of 49. I had always thought heart attacks happened to people who were old and overweight, not to people like my dad, who went with me to ball games and boxing matches and to the bars afterward. He had heart bypass surgery and eventually recovered, but I never did.

That November I turned 30, and it hit me hard. I could still remember the slogan that my generation had adopted back in the '60s, "Never trust anyone over 30." I had crossed the line, and was now one of them. I was no longer a kid who could still get away with acting like one. Whether I was ready or not, 30 meant having to stop being a kid and start acting like an adult. And my dad having a heart attack at such a young age left a lasting imprint on me that made me feel vulnerable instead of invincible. Turning 30 would have a dramatic impact on me.

It was a few months later, New Year's Day of 1979, to be exact, that an event occurred that would change the course of my life. It had snowed heavily the day before, something like 18 inches, but I was bound and determined to make it to the Regan's house for the New Year's Eve party. I managed to pick up our babysitter, who lived about three miles away, and Mimi and I headed across town to the party. The roads were treacherous and it took us forever to get there. We ended up getting back home around 4 A.M., and the babysitter needed to be home early, so after getting only a few hours sleep, I got dressed and headed out to take her home. About half a mile from her house the car got stuck in the snow. I asked her to take over the wheel and steer while I pushed, but she refused, saying that she didn't have a license or permit to drive and could get in trouble, and decided to walk the rest of the way home.

That's when it happened. While trying to push the car out of the snow bank, I could feel my heart suddenly stop, followed by rapid, pounding beats. The pattern continued for several minutes. I began to panic. I was convinced I was having a heart attack, just like my dad, and because of the weather, there was no one driving by who could help me. I sat in the car for a few minutes praying that either my heartbeats would return to normal or that someone would come by to help. As I sat there a I began experiencing a multitude of symptoms in addition to the irregular heartbeats, such as pounding head and chest, shortness of breath, upset stomach, numbness and tingling in my hands and feet, lightheaded, and an overwhelming sense of impending doom.

Eventually, a man came out of his house and helped me

get the car unstuck. I was able to make it back home, visibly shaken.

"Something's wrong with me," I said to Mimi when I walked in the door and explained what happened.

"Little wonder," she replied. "You drank 20 beers and got three hours sleep. Go back to bed. You'll be OK."

But I wasn't OK. The irregular heart beats continued as I laid in bed, scaring me more each time they happened.

And to make matters worse, Mimi was scheduled to go to work in a few hours, leaving me alone to watch the boys. I begged her not to go, that I was really worried something serious was wrong with me, and wanted her to stay home. But she said she had no choice and ended up going.

I couldn't call my doctor since it was a holiday, so I decided to call the emergency room at the hospital and explain my symptoms. The person who answered the phone said she would relay the information to a doctor and he would call me back.

The doctor returned my call about an hour later and was able to relieve my mind somewhat by telling me that I was most likely experiencing heart palpitations, which were probably the result of a combination of too much alcohol in my system, along with not getting enough sleep, and over exerting myself by trying to push the car out of the snow. He said after a good night's sleep the palpitations would likely stop, along with all my other symptoms, and I would be fine.

When Mimi got home from work I went to bed and eventually was able to fall asleep. When I woke up the next morning my symptoms were gone as the doctor had predicted. However, as soon as I got in the car and started driving to work on the snow packed roads the symptoms immediately returned. I turned the car around and headed back home.

"It's happening again," I said to Mimi, in a total state of panic. "I can't go to work. Something is wrong with me." I called my doctor and got in that day to see him. After checking me out and performing an EKG, he said there was nothing wrong with my heart. As soon as he told me that the symptoms began to decrease, and I felt much better. That was until I got back in the car and started driving home.

The pattern would continue for the next several days. Convinced there was still something wrong with my heart, I decided to go to the hospital to have a stress test and another EKG from a different doctor. Again, the diagnosis was the same. There was nothing wrong with my heart. But every time the symptoms would return I became more convinced that the doctors were wrong.

I began to live my life like an old man with a heart condition. I quit playing park board league basketball, something I had enjoyed doing for years, along with tennis, softball, volleyball, running, and anything that could put a strain on my heart. I had to force myself to go to work, especially in bad weather, in order to keep from losing my job. But out of town trips soon became impossible for me to go on without triggering a panic attack, and Mimi and the boys would often end up going without me.

We moved out of our house in the summer of 1979 and into a larger and nicer one in a better neighborhood. We also bought a second car that year. Meanwhile, I continued to slide downhill. For the next three years my life basically consisted of listening to my heartbeats, with nearly every skipped beat triggering a panic attack and all the physical symptoms that went with it. When I did venture out to the grocery store, the barber shop, a restaurant, or the mall and felt my heart skipping beats, my inclination was to escape and return home. Soon I began avoiding going to those places where I had suffered a panic attack, fearing that it would trigger another one.

Then one day in 1982 while at work, I started reading a pamphlet in the cafeteria entitled ***Prisoners of Fear***. It didn't take long for me to realize it was describing the last three years of my life. It talked about people who experienced a traumatic episode that triggered a panic attack, detailing every symptom that I had felt, from pounding head and heart, palpitations, dizziness, numbness, hyperventilation, and a sense of dread that something horrible was about to happen. It went on to say that after experiencing such an episode, if the person found himself in a similar situation, it would often automatically set off another attack, and that person would eventually begin to avoid those situations in order to prevent further attacks. There was even a term for it,—agoraphobia. The pamphlet concluded that most people who suffer from these attacks are convinced there is something wrong with them physically. But despite the frightening symptoms that occur during an attack, agoraphobia is a mental condition, not a physical one, that the symptoms, even the heart palpitations, were not life threatening, and that in time one could learn to deal with the panic attacks.

I was ecstatic to the point of tears. The doctors were right after all. My heart was fine. It was all in my head. I went to the library after work and picked up everything I could find relating to panic disorders and agoraphobia. I would cure myself and be back to normal in no time.

But I soon found out that it wasn't going to be as easy as I thought. The attacks kept coming, when would I board an airplane, or drive out of town on a trip, or even in a crowded elevator or movie theater. I tried to convince myself each time that it was all in my mind and that I was all right, but the attacks were as strong as ever, and left me confused and frightened. Apparently it had become so ingrained in my mind over the past three years that I was unable to control it from happening.

I started taking tranquilizers and drank to calm my nerves. I would do anything and take anything if it meant avoiding another panic attack. For the next several years, I basically lived in my own world, unable to overcome my disorder, and thinking of little else but myself.

In the winter of 1983, Mimi surprised me by informing me she was pregnant. On May 14th, 1984, our third son, Brian Andrew, was born. My initial reaction was, given my condition, that the last thing I needed was having another child in the house. But Brian proved to be good therapy for me. I made up my mind after we brought him home that I wasn't going to continue to live the rest of my life this way, that I would do whatever it took to try and get back to normal again, both for my sake and the sake of my family.

I decided to seek the help of a psychiatrist. After explaining what I had been through over the past five years, he agreed that I did indeed display the classic symptoms of agoraphobia. He went on to say that for most people it was a spiraling effect that eventually left many housebound, afraid to step out their front door.

"So what can I do to avoid being one of those people?" I asked.

"Well, there are medications available that help somewhat, but my personal recommendation is to try a technique called 'flooding' and use 'props' when you need them to help you get through the attacks," he said.

I was familiar with those terms, having read about them in one of the many books on the subject. "Flooding" is basically forcing one's self to get though the situation instead of avoiding it. And "props" is a term for doing something to make the person feel more at ease in order to help get through the situation.

"I need to warn you that it's going to be difficult, especially at first," he said. "A lot of people give up and aren't able to improve. You will most likely be susceptible to this condition the rest of your life, but if you stick with it long enough, the panic attacks will eventually lessen in intensity to the point where you will be able to cope with them."

I made up my mind from that day on that I was going to stop avoiding things and start doing them, no matter what the consequences. Soon I was starting to feel like a part of the family again, going on trips and events, and fighting through the panic attacks as best I could. The props that helped me get through situations were to do things like sit in the back of a theater or a social event where I felt like I could easily escape at the first onset of a panic attack. Or I would take the stairs instead of the elevator whenever possible.

As for out of town trips, I would do all of the driving to make sure we got directly to our destination without any side trips or delays, and leave when I said it was time to go. For the most part, my family, even though they could not understand what I was going through, went along with me without complaining, which provided a tremendous help in my recovery.

Little successes helped give me the confidence to carry on. I wrote a poem about Mike's first day at school, which was published in the local newspaper, and also received an award in a poetry contest. But the part I was most proud of was a letter I received from a person whom I had never met, telling me it was one of the most heartfelt and beautiful poems she had ever read, and that she would give it to her son to read when he sent his child off to school.

And I served as master of ceremonies for two years at the 20 Year Club at Bituminous, which was something every member was eventually called upon to serve for a two year stint. I not only enjoyed it, but was deeply touched afterward when I received many e-mails telling me how good a job I did, and even hearing from the committee that there were a lot of requests that I stay on and do it every year.

I even enjoyed my "15 minutes of fame" during this time in my life. My friend John and I heard that Muhammad Ali, one of our favorite athletes of all time, was going to be in the Quad Cities in a conference room at a hotel to campaign for a politician. We decided to go, of course only caring about the chance to see "The Greatest," rather than the politician, whose name I don't even recall.

We got to the hotel that night with the hopes of just catching a glimpse of our hero. Little did we realize what was to follow.

The place was packed of course, with hundreds of guys like us there to see Ali. After introducing his politician friend and giving a speech on stage, he started walking around the room amongst his many admirers. He was still fighting during those days, and even though he was nearing the end of his career, still looked in great shape, and the gleam in his eyes and the infectious smile that were a part of his trademark were still there. As he approached us, he stopped and looked directly at me, and said, "You look to be about my size, want to go a couple rounds?"

He started jabbing at me, actually striking me several times in rapid succession, (playfully of course), while I stood there in stunned amazement. The same left hand that had battered the likes of Joe Frazier and George Foreman was now pounding my chest with rapid jabs so fast that I couldn't even put up my hands in time to protect myself. He shook my hand afterward and signed an autograph. I looked over at my friend John, whose jaw was dropped wide open.

"I wish I would have brought my camera along," he said. "No one is going believe this. I can't even believe it, and I was standing there watching the whole thing."

Needless to say, it was night I will never forget.

I was starting to show signs of improvement. There would still be many setbacks, but I was determined more than ever to overcome my disorder.

Meanwhile, Mimi had her share of problems along the way too. Only hers were physical. I recall an afternoon when she was on her way to work and the three boys and I were watching a game on TV when we heard this thumping sound on the stairs leading into the garage, followed by moaning.

Brian got out of his chair and leaned over the railing.

"Mom's hurt," he said. We then all ran to the top of the stairs and saw Mimi lying at the bottom, rolling in pain. She had fallen half way down the stairs and twisted her ankle.

"I'm OK," she said, in typical Mimi fashion. "I think I can still make it to work." And she did.

And there was the time I was driving home from the grocery store and saw Mimi driving past me going the other direction. We both pulled over along the side of the road, and I got out, asking her where she was going.

"I think I might need to go to the hospital," she said, holding a blood filled wash cloth to her chin.

"Let me see," I said.

As she removed the wash cloth I saw her chin had split open, and I could actually see bone.

"Yes, you need to go the hospital," I said. "I will meet you there after I put the groceries away." Actually I needed to go home and lay down for a few minutes to keep from passing out.

Apparently she was attempting to straighten out Mike's bed frame, which was crooked to the point where the mattress wouldn't fit on the frame. When she went to unscrew the frame from the headboard, it broke loose, hitting her on the chin and knocking her unconscious. After a few minutes, she came to, with her chin gushing blood. There was no one around to help her, so she grabbed a wash cloth, held it tightly to her chin, and headed for the hospital. It took several stitches but she eventually recovered.

Then a few years ago, Mimi was involved in a serious car accident on her way to work. While heading through an intersection, she was run into by an oncoming pickup truck. The nurse called me from the hospital to tell me what happened, and, as usual, Mimi wanted to make sure I wouldn't worry, and talked to me over the phone, telling me she was OK, even though the collision rendered her unconscious. To this day she is still unable to recall the accident. The only thing she remembers is being taken to the hospital in an ambulance.

Despite her setbacks, Mimi continued to keep a positive outlook on life, and at the same time, tried her best to encourage me to do the same.

Chapter 11

~

By the late '80s the panic attacks had started to diminish in severity, as my doctor had predicted. But unfortunately, because of the way I had trained my mind to think, life for the most part had become something to get through rather than enjoy. In trying to cure my agoraphobia, I came to the realization that I had traded one problem for several others.

In order to get through stressful situations, I needed to feel like I was in complete control. And when I wasn't, I worried.

I would worry about anything that could go wrong, things like running late, or making a wrong turn during a trip, or getting stuck in traffic, having car problems, or getting sick while out of town. Soon I found myself worrying about everything, from my health, to my job, to even the weather. While I felt I was making some headway regarding the panic attacks, I disliked the person I was becoming, and wanted nothing more than to feel normal again.

Without realizing it, I had gradually transformed myself into a chronic worrier and a control freak. One of the things I regretted most was that my sons knew me only as the person I had become, and not the one I used to be. It also put tremendous pressure on Mimi, who had known both persons, and has described me as having gone from one extreme to the other, always hoping that someday I would reach a happy medium.

Our youngest son Brian turned out to be a great kid from the day he arrived. He was fun to be around and seldom got into trouble at home or school. Because he was so much younger than his older brothers, there wasn't the sibling rivalry between them like there was between Matt and Mike. They seemed to enjoy having him around as much as Mimi and I did. Brian rarely argued or threw temper tantrums. He was a happy kid, content with life.

One story I will always remember that describes Brian perfectly was the night that he and I were at home alone, with Mimi at work and his brothers off somewhere with their friends, and I asked him what he wanted to do.

"Could we watch *Beauty and the Beast*?" he said, a movie we had purchased that he had seen several times before, but one that I had never seen.

"Sure," I replied, not really wanting to watch it, but agreeing to sit down and see it with him.

After about 10 minutes or so into the movie, and noticing he was fully engrossed in it, I quietly left the room, and did some things, thinking he wouldn't even realize I was gone.

I finally came back about half an hour later only to realize that, without having said a word the whole time I was gone, he had paused the movie, just waiting for me to return.

Needless to say we watched the rest of it together.

But Brian would get even with me a few years later when I wanted him to watch a movie I liked called **55 Days at Peking**. I had tried for years in vain to get Matt and Mike interested in the classic historical epic movies, and also in Irish music, two of my great loves, but neither one would have anything to do with them. In fact, whenever I would play Irish music on the stereo in the living room, they would tell me they couldn't stand that noise and to put on the headphones. Brian was my last hope to try and convert, and one night when he had nothing better to do, agreed to watch the movie with me.

About 15 minutes into it I turned to him to tell him something historically significant about the movie, only to see that he had fallen asleep. And it wasn't that he had drifted off for a moment. He was dead to the world, with head back, mouth wide open, and snoring. I still tease him about that night, telling him that he has seen 'One' Day At Peking, and still has 54 more to go.

Brian was also a pet lover growing up, owning parakeets, hamsters, goldfish and a guinea pig named "Magic." He loved to go to pet stores, and hold and pet the animals, like rabbits, kittens and puppies.

Our family owned three dogs, (and no cats), over the years that we purchased from the Humane Society. Our first dog was a friendly little puppy when we first got him, who we named Ali, after my favorite fighter. The name fit him perfectly, as he quickly grew into a large dog who was too rough around the kids. After a year or so we gave him away to some people who were willing to take him.

A few years later we purchased a Beagle that reminded me of my old dog Pokey. We named him Patches. And. Like Pokey, Patches eventually became fat and lazy, content to lie around the house and do nothing. He was a good family dog, and lived out a long life according to dog years before developing a tumor, and having to be put to sleep.

Our third dog became our favorite. Mimi and the boys got him one day while I was at work. They named her Kirby, and when I first saw her she looked like a cross between a small deer and a large rat, with large pointy ears and long skinny tail. But she soon grew into a normal looking dog, and didn't become fat and lazy. Kirby was an active dog who would run around the back yard for hours, guarding our fence line as if to protect us from harm.

She was not only loyal, she was smart. We taught Kirby many tricks, such as fetching a tennis ball. One of our favorite games during the fall was to build a large pile of leaves and then throw the ball into the middle of it, telling Kirby to go get it. She would burrow her way into the pile of leaves and somehow manage to find the ball every time and retrieve it.

We taught her the usual dog tricks, such as shaking hands, rolling over, and giving kisses. I also taught her to chase squirrels out of our yard on command. She would spot one, and stand ready to pounce as soon as I gave the signal. "Get 'em, Kirb," I would say, and off she shot, chasing the squirrel out of the yard.

I also taught her to howl on command. I would start out making small howling noises and soon, with her head back, she would howl away and continued until I gave the command to stop.

The most amazing thing about Kirby was that she seemed

to have a built-in clock in her head. If we left the house for a half hour or so she would greet us at the door, tail wagging, and happy to see us, but then would go lay down somewhere. If we were gone for several hours, Kirby would jump up on us, and run around for a several minutes, obviously ecstatic. And if we gone overnight, she would run down the steps to the door upon our return, screaming and howling, jumping into our laps, and generally going berserk.

We had suspected for some time that when we weren't paying attention or weren't around, Kirby would jump up on our dining room table and eat what ever was left over after we had finished our meal. One day I decided to prove it. I placed our camcorder on the counter so it faced in the direction of the dining room table. We purposely left some food on our plates after we were done eating dinner, turned on the camcorder, and went into the garage, got in the car, and drove around for a few blocks. When we got home we definitely noticed some food missing, and put the videotape in the TV to watch what had transpired while we were gone.

Sure enough, as soon as Kirby heard the garage door close, she jumped up on one of the chairs, and then onto the table, and roamed around picking away at everyone's plates. The best part was when she heard the garage door open a few minutes later, her ears perked up, and she leaped from the table, causing a loud thud. We couldn't see exactly what happened, because it was out of the camera's view, but obviously in her haste to get down, Kirby had missed the chair. By the time we had gotten out of the car and up the stairs, she was lying comfortably on the sofa, as if nothing had happened.

Kirby had been housebroken for years, and was normally very good about letting us know when she needed to go out.

But after a while, she began losing control and going in the house. At first we reprimanded her, but after taking her to the vet for a checkup, we found out she had developed cancer of the bladder. The vet told us there was nothing we could do for her, and that it would only get worse in time.

After 10 years, Kirby had become a part of our family. We loved her and she loved us in return. But she continued to deteriorate, and we had to make the decision to have her put down.

I will never forget coming home from work the day of the scheduled procedure, and seeing Kirby sitting in the back yard with Mimi. Despite no doubt feeling ill and in pain, Kirby perked up her ears as soon as she saw me, and wagged her tail, as always, happy to see me. Although instead of running toward me like she usually did, she ambled slowly for a few steps, and then sat back down. I went over to her and petted her.

I wasn't sure which made me sadder, knowing we were seeing Kirby for the last time, or her not knowing. In either case, I could not bring myself to take her to the vet. Mimi volunteered to do it. Tears welling in my eyes, I couldn't say goodbye. I just looked at her one last time, and turned and went for a walk, recalling all the memories, and the happiness she had given our family over the years.

I continued to work for Bituminous as a computer programmer for 25 years, and planned on retiring there. However, one day I was handed something that I would not be able to cope with,—a pager.

They had hired a new manager in the mid '90s, and one of his requirements was that programmers were responsible for being on call at night, and solving any problems that came up. We started on a rotation basis, with one programmer being on call for one week at a time. At first it wasn't too bad, since there were eight programmers who were considered experienced enough for "beeper duty," as we called it.

However, within time, programmers began leaving the company for various reasons, and were replaced with inexperienced people who were unqualified to be on call at night. At one point we were down to three programmers on rotation, meaning that I was on call once every three weeks.

I was getting calls more frequently, sometimes late at night, which often involved me having to go into work in order to solve the problem. And even when the pager did not go off, I felt extremely uncomfortable, knowing that I could be called at a moment's notice any time during the night.

Eventually, it got to the point where I couldn't handle it anymore, and left Bituminous for a job in Cedar Rapids, Iowa, as a contract programmer.

After one year my contract expired and I wound up working for Pearson in Iowa City as a software developer, beginning in August of 1999. I worked there for nearly 10 years, making the 60 mile drive between Davenport and Iowa City every day.

In addition to writing short stories, articles, and poems in my spare time, I also became a list maker, ranking such things as my favorite movies, favorite songs, things I liked, and things I disliked. I don't know if that's something people do in their older age or if was just me.

Being a movie lover, I have seen many great films over the years. To me the greatest movie ever made is *Lawrence of Arabia*. *Braveheart* and *Forrest Gump* are also right up there. But in selecting a true top 10, my criteria was not necessarily the best movies I ever saw, but rather those that I would watch over and over again. Like when you're channel surfing and catch a movie halfway through and can't resist watching the rest of it, even though you've seen it a dozen times. Movies like **Caddyshack** and **Animal House**, which didn't quite make the top 10, but are classics none the less.

So with all due respect to the historical epics of the '60s, (especially **El Cid**), my top 10 favorite movies are:

1) *The Right Stuff*
2) *Hoosiers*
3) *Die Hard*
4) *The Great Escape*
5) *On Golden Pond*
6) *Cinderella Man*
7) *Heaven Can wait*
8) *Planes, Trains, and Automobiles*
9) *O Brother Where Art Thou*
10) *Tombstone*

And with all due respect to the Irish, my top 10 songs are:
1) *Hallelujah* (from the movie **Shrek)**
2) *Sounds of Silence*
3) *House of the Rising Sun*
4) *Blowing in the Wind*
5) *Walking In Memphis*
6) *City of New Orleans*
7) *Goodbye Yellow Brick Road*
8) *True Companion*
9) *April Come She Will*
10) *Sweet Baby James*

The top 10 things I like:
1) Autumn
2) Playing golf well
3) Ancient Irish folk music
4) Tailgating at football games
5) Sitting outside on a beautiful evening
6) Watching sports on TV
7) Writing
8) Looking at old family photographs
9) Bagpipes
10) Cheeseburgers

And the top 10 things I dislike:
1) Winter
2) Playing golf poorly
3) Having to wait in line
4) Raking leaves
5) Impatient drivers
6) Four way stops
7) Elevators
8) The telephone
9) Traffic jams
10) Rainy Mondays

Actually I find myself making lists of nearly everything, from my favorite sports, to my favorite months of the year, to my favorite foods. It either goes hand in hand with my penchant for writing, or I have become delusional.

I even made a list of my favorite holidays. When I was a kid, Christmas would have been number one, but now it's pretty far down on my list, mostly due to the fact that I am a terrible gift giver. Mimi has a knack for picking out the perfect gift for me every Christmas, while I seem to always get her something that she ends up not liking and eventually returning. And with the exception of setting up the Christmas tree and helping hang the outdoor lights, my only obligation is buying her a gift. Normally I wait until the last minute, rush out to the mall only to fight traffic for an hour, spend another half hour trying to find a parking place, and wander around aimlessly among a thousand other guys doing the same thing as me, looking for a gift, any gift, for my wife, that I hope she will like, and then spending another hour in line waiting to pay for it.

But there was one Christmas that I thought was going to be different. My mom gave me a tip on what to get for Mimi, sure that she was going to love it, and the best part was that I didn't even have to go the mall to get it. She said it was in the East Village, a tiny section of town with only a handful of stores, at a place called Isabel Bloom's. All I had to do was drive over there, pick out a statue called "Comfort," and be home in time for the big game.

I was somewhat familiar with the works of Isabel's, with Mimi having purchased some of her items over the years. To me they just looked like pieces of concrete formed into various shapes that were supposed to resemble things, but if that was going to make her happy, then I was all for it.

As I approached the shop I pictured in my mind a sweet little old lady sitting in a rocking chair, chiseling away at her concrete statues. I figured she would be so happy to see a customer, she might even offer me milk and cookies.

When I walked in I was greeted by a woman all right, but when I asked her if she was Isabel, she just smiled, with a look on her face like I was some sort of idiot.

She asked me if there was something in particular I was looking for.

"Comfort," I said confidently, trying to show her that I knew exactly what I was doing.

The woman pointed to one of the statues on the wall and told me that was it.

"Great," I said. "I'll take it. Please wrap it up and I'll be on my way."

The woman gave me that same smile again, which by now had become annoying. "You will need to stand in that line, sir, and tell the person at the desk which item you would like to purchase."

"Line?" I said, my voice cracking.

She pointed to the back of the room. That's when I saw it. A line of people as far as the eye could see. Suddenly the little shop in the Village became the Little Shop of Horrors.

"What are all these people doing here?" I said, as I began to break out into a cold sweat.

Again with the smile she replied, "We're very popular this time of year. Didn't you know?"

The shrieking violin music from *Psycho* began playing in my head, as I started to hyperventilate, and needed to escape immediately. But as I tried to head for the exit, more people began pouring in, many wearing shirts that read, "I love Isabel," with a heart in place of the word love. I was trapped in Isabel hell.

I managed to escape and make my way back to the car, still visibly shaken from my first and last trip to the Village of the Damned.

"Maybe she could use a sweater," I thought to myself, as I headed for the mall.

Chapter 12

~

Whoever said, "Youth is wasted on the young" knew what they were talking about. If someone were to have asked me when I was 20 if I was happy, my answer would have been "I don't know, I never thought about it." It was only after I turned 30 and started experiencing problems that I realized how happy I once was.

I have spent the past 30 years of my life forcing myself to get through things, but along the way lost the ability to enjoy them. It would be an exaggeration to say that I have not enjoyed a single moment over those years, however. In fact, I made somewhat of a resurgence during the '90s. I went on family trips to places like Cape Cod, Charleston, South Carolina, San Francisco, LA, and New Orleans, something I wouldn't have been able to do 20 years ago.

I started playing basketball again, competing in something called "Hoopfest," a three on three street ball tournament, and took up tennis, softball and jogging again.

While I still had occasional moments of panic and anxiety, I had for the most part made significant improvement since those dark days in the '80s.

I have a lot to be thankful for. I love my wife, who has stuck by me through thick and thin, and helped me make it through the rough times with her always positive attitude. And I love my three boys, all of whom I am proud of.

Matt got married in 1998, and has two granddaughters whom I adore, and get to see often since they live in the area. Mike became a sports writer, first covering the San Francisco 49ers, then moved to New Orleans, and is currently covering the Saints. He got married in 2004, and recently had a grandson who we get see on occasion. Brian gained fame by helping the victims of Hurricane Katrina, and then writing an article about it which won the Hearst Foundation National Collegiate story of the year. He has also journeyed around the world on his own after graduating from college, and walked across the United States with a friend to meet and help out people along the way, and to show those who are leery of strangers that most people are kind and caring.

My dad passed away in 1986 from lung cancer. I visit his grave every Sunday, and tell him how much I miss him, and recall all the good times we spent together. We still talk about the Hawks and Cubs.

My mom retired recently from Von Maur department store, where she worked for nearly 40 years, and is now doing volunteer work at CASI, a center for active senior citizens. She was recently diagnosed with lymphoma, which has slowed her down somewhat, but she is able to go places and do things, and enjoys life to the fullest. In fact, both my mom and Mimi's mom remain remarkably active considering they are both in their '80s. They put me to shame. To them I probably seem like a young man. I envy them, and anyone who can find happiness in life at that age.

I gradually began to slow down as the years passed, and the aches and pains began to become more prevalent, and eventually I had to give up playing basketball and tennis, and go from jogging to walking.

Then in 2006 I began experiencing stomach pains, which gradually became more intense, and finally decided to make a doctor's appointment to get it checked out. But the week before my appointment, I had to be rushed to the hospital with what turned out to be a bleeding ulcer. I ended up having surgery, and spending nine days in the hospital. The doctor who treated me said it was from having taken too much aspirin over the years, which irritated my stomach lining, and eventually wore a hole through it. The only thing I was allowed to take for pain after that was Tylenol.

I spent a month off work, and the ordeal left me with psychological scars as well as physical ones. When I went back to work I had trouble concentrating on my job, and began having panic attacks, both while at work and sometimes on my way to work. I finally had to take medical leave for two weeks, during which time my doctor and I experimented with various anxiety medications to help me get back on my feet.

I finally found a medication which worked well enough to at least get me to and through work, but in the spring of 2008, I was to lose my job.

I was called into human resources one morning, March 4th

to be exact, having no idea what was about to come. I had no prior warning that I was doing poorly at work, with the exception of missing time due to my surgery and medical leave. My annual reviews weren't great, but there was no indication on the part of my manager that I was performing at an unacceptable level. Plus, there were no rumors circulating around the building of possible impending layoffs.

I was told by my manager that morning, along with a person from human resources, that I was part of a large layoff, that I would be escorted out of the building, and that someone would box up my personal belongings, and I was to pick them up the following day. That's all that was said.

Naturally, I was in a state of shock. I don't even remember driving home that morning. All I recall is walking in the door and having to tell Mimi the news.

Despite them telling me that I was part of a large layoff, I was pretty certain it was an excuse for my manager to get rid of an aging employee with medical problems. I thought about taking legal action, but decided it would be too hard to prove, since they were laying off other people during that time.

It was a tough age to be without a job. I was nearing 60, and was too old for anyone to want to hire me, and yet too young to retire. I was given severance pay and tried looking for a comparable job in the area, but nothing was available, not for me anyway. The only work I could find was a seasonal job at Super Target over the holidays, and have been unemployed ever since.

I spend my days looking through the help wanted ads in the paper, and on-line employment web sites, playing bad golf on occasion, doing yard work, mowing the lawn, helping my mom with her yard work, going for a three mile walk every day, taking frequent naps, Tylenol, and hot baths to soothe my aching joints.

I have taken up a new sport, thanks to Brian. He talked me into buying some Frisbee discs recently, and playing Frisbee golf, something he had played as a student in Iowa City. He is very good at it and I am horrible. But it's good exercise and gives us a chance to bond, which has become less frequent among my sons over the past few years, with Mike living in New Orleans, Brian traveling the world and now living in Chicago, and Matt having to work long hours at his job.

I have had a love-hate relationship with golf throughout my life, starting when my dad first taught me the game when I was a teenager. Naturally, I played poorly when I was first learning the game, but I enjoyed it and stuck with it, and began playing more and more when I was in my '20s. There was a time when I played at least once a week, sometimes more, and would hit buckets of balls on the driving range, and practice chipping in my back yard. I reached a point where I was consistently scoring in the high '70s to low '80s. I even made a hole in one once, with my boys as witnesses, and still have the scorecard.

Then as the years went by I began to play less, and my scores began to get worse. I became frustrated every time I played poorly, and couldn't deal with it mentally, even though I knew the reason was because I wasn't devoting as much time to the game.

I even quit playing entirely for several years, unable to cope with the fact that I wasn't playing as well as I used to. Eventually, I took it up again, trying to approach it with a different mindset, not caring about my scores anymore, and being content with just hitting a good shot every now and then. It's still a hurdle for me that I haven't completely cleared. Playing good golf is still more fun than playing bad, but I'm working on it. Most of the time I don't even keep score anymore.

Mowing the lawn is usually a pretty dull and simple task. However, I did mange to liven things up one day recently. While I was cutting the back yard, the mower ran out of gas. I went to fill it and accidentally spilled some gas on the engine, which was still hot from having been running. When I started it up, the mower caught on fire due to the excess gas that had I had spilled. The flame wasn't all that intense, but I was afraid to go near it, thinking the gas tank might explode. The only thing I could think to do was call 911.

Within five minutes two fire trucks pulled up in front of our house, followed by probably 30 kids on bikes who were excited to see what was going on. One of the firemen came around back and took a look at the situation. I heard one of his buddies yell from the truck, "Should I bring the hose around?"

"No, I got it," he replied, and put the fire out with an extinguisher he had brought with him. "Well, that's one way of getting out of mowing the lawn," he said.

Meanwhile the kids who had flocked into the back yard,

hoping to see something spectacular, were disappointed, and turned around and headed back home on their bikes.

Mimi had been out shopping, and as the fire trucks were leaving she was pulling into the driveway, and, naturally concerned, asked me what happened. After telling her the story she just rolled her eyes and said, "I'm not sure that qualifies as a 911 call. I would have just thrown a blanket over it or something."

The next day she was reading the newspaper and got to the emergency calls section.

"Oh, here's one that sounds pretty scary," she said sarcastically. "A lawn mower caught on fire at 1335 West 57th Street." I still hear about it from her to this day.

I managed to avoid ending up being housebound, like many people afflicted with agoraphobia, which is an accomplishment that I should be proud of. The trouble is, I don't feel like going out much anymore. I have become content to sit at home and watch movies on TV instead of going to the theater, and cooking at home instead of eating out at a restaurant. We get together with our friends once a month to play cards, a tradition we have kept up for nearly 30 years, and we all get together once a year to attend an Iowa football game. But otherwise I have become a homebody, much to the dismay of my wife, who loves to get together with friends and travel places.

I find myself spending a lot of my time reflecting back on the good old days. Despite not liking to travel, I will get the urge to drive to Dubuque every now and then and walk around the campus, reminiscing about my days at Loras, and then head over to Clarke, and reflect back to the times Mimi and I spent there together. And I spend many evenings when Mimi is at work looking through old family albums while listening to Irish music, with no one yelling at me to put on the headphones.

It's been a long time since my Superman days, and quite a while since I've felt like Superman. I now sit in my soft leather recliner, and sometimes wrap a blanket over me for warmth, where once a red cape draped my shoulders. And in place of the red "S" I once wore on my chest, I now sometimes draw an imaginary "O" for "Old Man."

I know that a lot of people believe that 60 is not that old, and will say such things to me like, "It beats the alternative," and, "You're only as old as you feel."

The trouble is I feel like crap. They teach you in school about math and history and science, but no one teaches you about how you're supposed to grow old and accept it when your mind and body start breaking down, and you can no longer do the things you once did.

Whoever coined the phrase "golden years" to describe being old is either the world's greatest optimist or someone trying to fool them self. There's nothing "golden" about it that I can see. Life to me is like a leaf on a tree. I starts out as a bud, (birth), then blossoms, (childhood), becomes full grown and green, (adolescence and early adulthood), then changes colors, (middle age), before withering and shriveling, (old age), and eventually falling off the tree and onto the ground, (death). Unlike life, a leaf gets to start over and do it all again. We only get one chance.

While others look forward to their later years as a time of

peace, comfort, and tranquility, getting to travel and visit their children and grandchildren, and walk arm in arm into the sunset, I can only envision doctors, and hospitals, and nursing homes, and attending funerals of friends and loved ones, and those who are left eventually attending mine.

What was once something that seemed far off into the future has become a reality that I now must confront. The combination of turning 60, losing my job the way I did, realizing no one is going to hire me for a comparable one, and the ever increasing signs that my mind and body are starting to deteriorate, have left me feeling disillusioned, bitter, despondent, frightened, and mostly, old. I have spent the past 30 years thriving on being in control. I have come to the realization that I am no longer in control of my life, that life is in control of me.

I fully realize that there are many people who have it worse than me, some of whom I know personally. People with terminal cancer, the handicapped, those who have lost a spouse or child, and elderly persons with no one to care for them, or care about them, all have it worse than I do. But despite that, I am still unable to change my attitude toward the way I feel.

I've often wondered why life, and the way we perceive it, works the way it does. Technically, young people should worry more than older people, yet it's the other way around. When you are young, you have your whole life ahead of you, and should take precautions to make sure nothing happens to you that would end your life prematurely. But when you grow old, you have experienced life, and have done most of the things life has to offer, and should be accepting of whatever happens and not worry about it.

Maybe it's because when you're young you feel invincible, capable of doing anything and everything without fear of the consequences. As you grow older, you feel more vulnerable, knowing that death is an unavoidable reality.

It's been 30 years since I've felt invincible. When I think back to all those times when I took chances and risked injury, and even death, without worrying about the consequences, I can only shake my head at how much I have changed, and reached the point where I am now.

As the aging process continues to take it's toll on me, I can only think of what lies ahead, and it's not a comforting feeling. I want to feel the way I used to. I don't want to be frightened of what the future holds. I want to look forward to it. I wish this story could have a happy ending, and that I could change my attitude about growing old. I am currently seeing another in the long list of psychiatrists, therapists, and counselors in the hope that one of them can tell me something different than all the others, something that will turn on a light and allow me to see things from a different perspective, and enable me to find, if not happiness, at least peace and contentment. If that were to happen I would be more than happy to write a sequel to this story, and entitle it something like "Loving Life After Sixty."

In fact, the counselor I am currently seeing said something recently that may prove to be the key to finally finding that elusive peace and contentment.

During our most recent consultation, he said to me, "Have you ever seen the movie *Office Space*?" to which I replied that I have seen it many times and that it was one of my favorite movies. The premise is that the main character, Peter, is an unhappy man who hates his job, worries that he will be stuck in it until he retires, is intimidated by his boss, is involved in a bad relationship with his girlfriend, and in general leads a miserable existence.

Then one night he is talked into going to see a hypnotherapist, and, through a bizarre turn of events, is transformed into a totally different person. He sleeps until noon the following day, even though he is supposed to be at work. He tells a co-worker when asked why he didn't show up, "Because I didn't feel like it." He sees his boss standing in the aisle the next day waiting to confront him about not showing up for work, and walks right past him without saying a word, leaving the boss speechless. He takes breaks whenever he wants, comes and goes when he pleases, and decides he is going to live his life the way he wants from now on instead of the way others expect him to.

"My advice to you," said my counselor, "is to live your life like Peter from now on."

I couldn't believe what I was hearing. Instead of the usual advice such as relaxation techniques, self help videos and CDs, meditation, and deep breathing exercises, a professional counselor was actually advising me to act like a character out of a movie. It clicked. I immediately felt an overwhelming sense of liberation and relief. It was like telling someone who has spent the past 30 years swimming upstream against the current to just lay in a raft and let everything go, and just float along with the current, without a care in the world.

When I left the office that day and got to the parking lot I noticed a line of traffic backed up due to road construction.

My immediate response was a typical one, to get angry and upset. But then I stopped and asked myself, "What would Peter do in this situation?"

I got in my car, took out an Irish CD, and cranked it up to full volume, tapping my hands and feet to the rhythm of the music, and smiling as I slowly moved along with the rest of the traffic. I'm sure people who were looking at me probably thought I was crazy, but I didn't care. I was in my world, not theirs. Soon the traffic cleared, and I was on my way. I had managed to turn a negative moment into a positive one, which is exactly what my counselor was trying to teach me.

I don't know whether I can undo the way I have trained my brain to think over the past 30 years, but I'm certainly going to give it a shot.

What the future holds for me I do not know. I could die tomorrow, or I could live for another 30 years. What I do know after having left his office that day is how I live out the remainder of my life is up to me, and that it is possible to change, even at 60. Only time will tell whether I can turn things around.

But for now, sitting in my recliner and watching a Cubs game on TV, my thoughts turn back to that day my dad first took me to Wrigley Field. I fight back a tear, recalling those early days and the fond memories I will always keep in my heart of a boy growing up.